Happiness comes in m[...]

In the company of good fr[...]

In the feeling you get when you make another [...]

or in the promise of hope renewed

it is ok to let yourself be happy

because you never know how fleeting that happiness may be

be happy for above all else you deserve the world

love you

_____

I believe in following this you will
find a part of yourself long forgotten

Mind, Body, Soul Journal

Mind, Body, Soul Journal

Discover a sense of purpose and live your best life

ANDREA HAYES

THE BESTSELLING AUTHOR OF *My Life Goals Journal*

GILL BOOKS

Gill Books
Hume Avenue
Park West
Dublin 12
www.gillbooks.ie

Gill Books is an imprint of M.H. Gill and Co.

© Andrea Hayes 2018

978 07171 8347 0

Designed by Tanya M Ross, www.elementinc.ie
Edited by Emma Dunne
Proofread by Ellen Christie
Printed by BZ Graf, Poland

All photos courtesy of unsplash.com
This book is typeset in Freight 10pt.

A CIP catalogue record for this book is available from the British Library.

5 4 3 2

To Jen

I will never understand your fascination with writing but what i do understand now is the fact that somehow you have found inner strength from somewhere. today i literally watched a barrister deliver bad news to you and you were inconsoleable. and then an hour later you found the strength to laugh and smile in the shopping Centre with Laura and myself. you are my hero. an inspiration in a place i never believed was there. i cant count the times over the last two years that you have not made me so proud and impressed so much. you will never realise how much i actually love you because our history is so as it is but never more than now to i realise the positive impact on my life it has been watching you battle your demons. this has really put my small issues into perspective. when it comes to you i just love how everyone gravitates towards you without you even knowing it. i love watching your reaction as you get small simple presents and i know the next few months might be difficult but i believe you writing down might be a small help. because however little it may be. well it may help. i found my soulmate before size. even knew i existed & when i managed to finally get you alone I have loved you since the very first calamitious date in your house. words shall never do justice my thoughts on you but actions will and as long as this case is ongoing you have my undivided moments & im here whenever you need to call, text or meet and thats a promise. after that i cannot promise i.ll be readily available as Hank wants to kill ha_ I love you now, then and forever. I cant wait to see you grow over the next decade my beautiful gorgeous friend   —

To Skylar because it is happening

Chris ♡xxx

Acknowledgements

I have been wondering where this book sprang from. I suppose it was a deep yearning to create balance and harmony in my life that led me on a search to find my own unique blend of spirituality. The thoughts and ideas you will read have been composed mostly from trusting that a higher power was guiding me, and also from wonderful learning experiences and teachers who have helped me on my path.

All of those encounters needed to be woven together with creativity and action and that happened because of the patience, grace and guidance of my brilliant editor Sarah Liddy; over many enlightening conversations with Sarah, this journal became a reality. The completion of this book was eased by the support of the stellar team at Gill: there are so many people who work on a book without any applause so I want to wholeheartedly acknowledge Sheila, Tanya, Teresa, Ellen, Seán, Paul, Linda and all the team – you are truly amazing and I am so grateful to you all.

Thank you to the utterly inspiring and brilliant Norah Casey, my great TV3 colleague Alan Hughes, my dearest friends Helen Goldin and Patrick Bergin, the ever-positive Paul Congdon, and – a beautiful person inside and out – author Claudia Carroll for her generous words of support and kindness.

There are so many people who have kept my light bright during this writing journey, particularly Fr Myles O'Reilly and my soul friends in Anamcharadas. I am blessed to have so many 'radiators' in my life (you will read about them later in the journal) and it feels almost impossible to mention everyone who has inspired me. So to anyone who has reached out and been a part of my life in any small way or is a lifelong friend – thank you. I am so grateful to my loving family Lavinia, Maria, Brian, mum Marie, Mary and Pat.

I have to give special mention to my squad of cheerleaders: my best pal, mentor and PR queen Valerie Roe; Teresa Murray for the endless advice and keeping the G&Ts flowing; Vanessa Fox O'Loughlin from writing.ie for the hours of writing chats in Whelan's wine bar; and not forgetting the Jonny Cooper Appreciation Group (you know who you are!).

My biggest supporter is my wonderful husband David Torpey, and together with the love and laughter of my daughters Brooke and Skylar and our dog Dash, life is pretty amazing.

Finally, I want to thank you, the reader. Whoever or wherever you are reading these words, may you be blessed with blessings and abundance as you go in the direction of your true calling in this life.

Live your best life.

'We should be in harmony
with our own consciousness;

OUR MIND, BODY AND SOUL SHOULD BE
ONE IN INTEREST AND IN PURPOSE.

And in that unified condition, we can actually
express that natural innate love that

WE HAVE FOUND IN OUR OWN LIFE IN
EVERYTHING WE DO IN THE WORLD.'

– Radhanath Swami

A MESSAGE FROM ANDREA

Have you ever wanted to make changes in your life?
Do you want deepen your sense of purpose and find more
meaning and fulfilment amidst the chaos of the daily grind?

Deep within, is there a voice gently telling you that there is more for you to do in this life, an untapped potential you need to discover?

Do you feel you are missing your calling?

Have you answered yes to any of the above, but when you try to start making some positive changes in your life, you find yourself too exhausted to even think about it? Or paralysed by fear? Or maybe you just don't know what to focus on first?

THE POWER OF JOURNALING

A journal is not only a great place to write your innermost feelings and record quotes or sayings that inspire you, but also a wonderful tool to help you analyse and figure out where you are in your life at this present moment, where you want to go and, importantly, what your life purpose truly is.

When embracing change, a journal can be a great place to start. Think of the pages within the *Mind, Body, Soul Journal* as signposts, pointing you in the right direction. But it's up to you to be clear about your purpose and to follow a definite path to help you describe and capture your journey. The helpful meditations will be a wonderful tool to guide your progress.

My journaling story started almost 30 years ago, and I have been keeping diaries, notebooks and journals for as long as I can remember. I have always considered the act of writing down my most personal experiences at the end of each day to be a form of therapy, and it has definitely helped me through life's many ups and downs. But, more importantly, it has really helped me in managing my health challenges, namely a brain disorder, diagnoses of Chiari Malformation 1, Spinal Stenosis, POTS and mild EDS, all of which cause daily chronic pain.

In 2013, a life-changing medical diagnosis inspired me to make some big changes in my life. I took time out from work commitments to become the best version of myself that I could be.

During this time, I made it my intention to prioritise my health and wellness and began to take excellent care of my body. I embraced one of the most powerful lessons from the ancient science of Ayurveda and began to see my body as my temple. I learned how to become an empowered patient and really understand my own body and my ability to live a happy life despite the pain.

Instead of focusing on the constant pain and what my body couldn't do, I started to become more and more appreciative of what my body was doing for me. I adopted new healthy routines to ensure proper maintenance, regular attention and gentle pacing so my body would be the best it could be. What I learned from this informed my first book, *Pain-Free Life: My Journey to Wellness*.

Sometimes a book can send your life in a new direction – this certainly happened to me. You might be familiar with the phrase 'When life hands you lemons, make lemonade', coined by Norman Vincent Peale, who published his bestselling book, *The Power of Positive Thinking*, in 1952. It spent over 150 weeks in the bestseller lists and when I read it almost 50 years later, it had a profound effect on me and my life. However, my own journey to wellness went way beyond the power of positive thinking. Because I believed fully in the power of the mind to heal and attract great abundance in our lives, I decided to study clinical hypnotherapy and NLP (neuro-linguistic programming).

As a trained hypnotherapist, I learned all about the potential to achieve greatness within our own minds. Initially, I was only focused on how I could reprogram my mind to help ease my pain and how to create new neural pathways to retrain my brain to feel and interpret pain differently. But this quickly shifted as I realised the immense value in harnessing the power of the brain to help in goal setting and personal achievement.

THE IMPORTANCE OF SELF-AWARENESS

Many neuroscientists, athletes and world leaders have long supported the theory that understanding your subconscious mind is the key to success.

This is why writing down your goals every day, visualising your intended outcome and regularly saying affirmations are so important! I shared these ideas in my second book, *My Life Goals Journal*, and shared my journey with so many of you who also found success by using the tools outlined.

My path to live a more fulfilling life continued and my search for knowledge never weakened. While studying the mind and the subconscious, I was fascinated by the idea that from the time of birth until eight years old, your mind is one big receptacle for everything you hear, say, see, dream or experience. When a child nears eight years old, the mind separates and organises into the conscious and unconscious mind, and a barrier is formed between the two. The child becomes 'aware'.

Experts agree that the conscious mind makes up less than 10 per cent of the mind. The subconscious, which is already full of subconscious programs by eight years old, makes up 90 per cent or more of the mind. Much of our behaviour and patterns, despite our conscious wishes, are a result of subconscious programming formed before we reached an age of awareness.

I wanted to really examine my own self-awareness, and discover what subconscious messages and self-limiting beliefs from childhood were hardwired into my consciousness potentially stopping me from being my true authentic limitless self.

I had many questions and this led me on a journey to really explore what past patterns or learned behaviours were blocking my path to being my true self. I began to look at my life through a new lens. I had spent a long time mastering my body and mind but I felt strongly that I needed a deep dive into my soul, my spirit, my self-awareness, my higher consciousness – whatever you want to call it.

I knew that to create more balance between my mind, body and soul and to achieve the enlightenment and true happiness I desired, I had to keep searching. This brought me on a spiritual journey, into an area of my life I felt was lacking – I wanted to give my spirit the same attention I had given my body and mind in recent years. For the first time, I saw the value in honouring my soul and spirit, as without that, I felt something was out of sync in my life.

Looking back, my longing for a deeper spiritual connection had grown stronger since I had become a mother. A childlike curiosity about all things faith-related can be a good way of getting a fresh perspective on your soul's journey in life.

I wanted to give my child a solid spiritual foundation on which to build her own future faith choices.

My husband has very different spiritual beliefs to me, so how do you find the middle ground in faith? For me, it is all about core values, which we both thankfully share. So we operate in a home of openness and acceptance. I teach my daughter my Christian values and my husband talks to her about science, evolution and the Big Bang, and together we foster respect for all religious and scientific beliefs.

MY BREAKTHROUGH MOMENT

Over the past two years I have been doing what many parents will relate to – as mothers, we are teachers, and I have been showing my young daughter how to make the sign of the cross before we start our daily prayer. Blessing yourself with the sign of the cross as you pronounce the names of the three Divine Persons of the Blessed Trinity is an ancient practice and prayer. The movement traces a cross over the body, and by using three fingers you represent the Father, the Son and the Holy Spirit.

I hadn't really noticed that many of us do this subconsciously almost every day or every week at mass, or even when passing a church or graveyard. It was only when I had to explain the practice to my daughter that I started to think more deeply about it. She understood little of the words we pronounced, and she had no awareness of this great mystery of our faith, so to try to make sense of it I explained that, like many other things, God is made up of different parts. She still looked puzzled so we took an apple as an example: it is made up of skin, the flesh inside and the seeds in the core; similarly liquid, vapour and ice are all water. Then, in a final bid to explain, I said that every person is made up of a mind, body and soul, and in many ways this is like God.

Our mind is like the Father, our body is like Jesus the Son and then our soul represents the Holy Spirit. Together, they make a Divine unit, which is our unique self, and that is the same as God our creator. I explained that God is in all of creation, we are all one. She asked me, in her childlike innocence, 'If God is in everyone then are we God?'

While explaining that we are not God but we are one with God, her comment stuck with me. There is a oneness with all of creation. I started to think more about the concept of a universal consciousness. Could her simplistic, childlike way of looking at it be true? Are we all Divine, with a higher power that is indeed within us? I began to question myself about my connection to God, and why, if I was made perfect in his likeness, didn't I see myself that way?

The notion stayed with me for a long time and eventually something shifted in how I saw the world. Although I was supposed to be teaching my daughter something, I had a moment of intense clarity and I wondered ...

Imagine for a second that we are the Divine – and that is the mystery of our faith: we need to have faith in ourselves. Could humanity and divinity be interconnected? Could knowledge and realisation could be the first step in the manifestation of who we really are? With the embracing of our divinity, could we create our own heaven on earth?

What if we believe anything is possible if we connect truly with our own true divinity? If we begin looking at the world through the lens of unconditional love, as we are told the Divine looks at all creation, what blessings and miracles could we encounter?

I wrote at length in my own journal about this idea and spoke to my spiritual companion about it. A spiritual companion is someone who listens and gently guides you on your own spiritual path. Many people develop some spiritual practices to feed their soul, such as going to church, praying, meditating, yoga, energy healing, tai chi or even journaling. Having a spiritual companion is another of these; he or she is someone who you can talk to about your sense of connection to your soul or a higher power and reflect on its role in your own life. I myself am a trained spiritual companion and Bethany grief minister and I studied for this while writing this journal.

'THE KINGDOM OF GOD
DOES NOT COME
WITH YOUR CAREFUL
OBSERVATION,
NOR WILL PEOPLE SAY, "HERE
IT IS" OR "THERE IT IS,"
BECAUSE THE KINGDOM
OF GOD
IS WITHIN YOU.'

– Luke 17:2

In recognition of the diverse ways people think of God, from now on I will talk about the **Divine**: this can mean a higher power, the creator, a universal consciousness, the universe, an energy or a power greater than ourselves, mother nature, a supreme being or deity, or some conception of God. The meaning of the Divine is for you to decide and it is personal to everyone, so from here on, you can imagine what Divine means to you.

Starting with the understanding that we begin with nothing and we leave with nothing, then we have nothing to lose or fear by striving to follow our dreams and live the life we truly desire. Maybe in order to align with our innate calling in this world and our own inner wisdom we need to find our true divinity, and a true union of the mind, body and soul that will indeed bring the spiritual freedom we crave and that pure, unconditional, loving relationship with the self, the universe and the Divine, as we are all one, all connected.

When we learn how to create harmony between our mind, body and soul, we not only feel in balance, but also feel that our lives have colour, passion and a sense of belonging: that's when we are truly living our life's purpose.

Andrea Hayes

'The world rewards you for what is in your mind,

THE UNIVERSE REWARDS YOU FOR WHAT IS IN YOUR HEART,

and the Heavens reward you for what is in your soul.'

– Matshona Dhliwayo

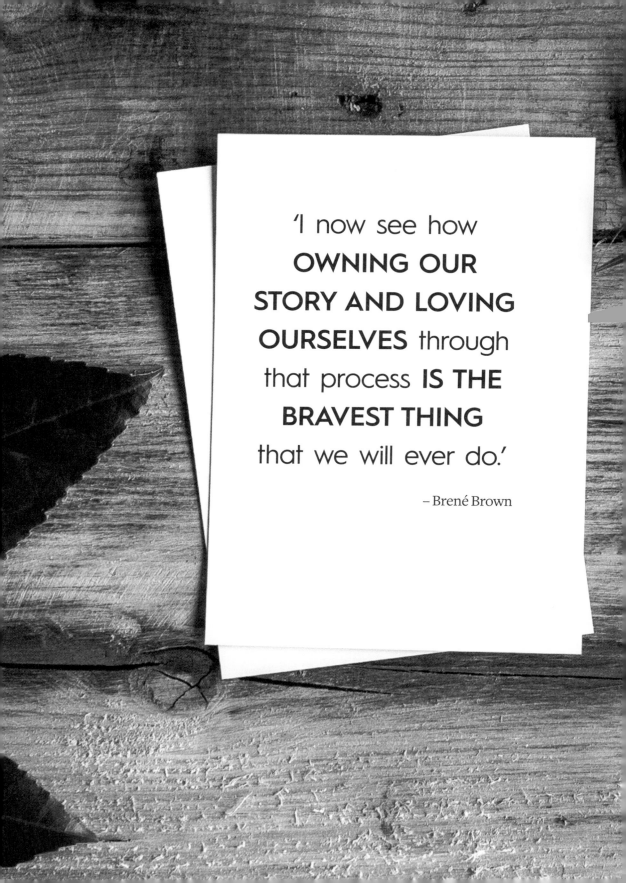

'I now see how **OWNING OUR STORY AND LOVING OURSELVES** through that process **IS THE BRAVEST THING** that we will ever do.'

– Brené Brown

How to Use the Mind, Body, Soul Journal

Each month is themed. You will be encouraged to make time for your own sacred space to follow the prompts and exercises in each chapter and answer the relevant **soul questions** to help you on your journey. This is a time to review what you have learned at the end of each theme.

It is also important to do separate journaling and use the meditations provided on my website (www.andreahayes.ie) written specifically for the themes of each month. I would recommend that you get a separate journal from this one to write at length about your experiences. Writing is very personal: some people like to write a lot, others just need to write a word or sentence to prompt them, and some are more comfortable writing in a digital format. Whatever works for you is what is best for you to do. The location where you write in it is just as unique as you, but I would recommend you have a separate place to write in this journal. You can mark it months 1 to 12 and follow the guidance on the pages that follow, and use it as an addition to the space left for writing in this book.

While I was on this journey, I used three separate journals – one for my mind, body and soul insights, one as a daily gratitude journal, and one as a dream journal.

'A personal journal is an ideal environment in which to "become". It is a perfect place for you to think, feel, discover, expand, remember, and dream.'

– Brad Wilcox

JOURNALING

Journaling is a life-long practice of mine, and it has inspired some of the most powerful insights into my own evolution and spiritual growth. In the following pages I will share snippets from my own one-year transformational journal experience. I cannot explain the phenomenon of my journal experience except to say this: it works for me, and I believe it can work for you too. Through using the *Mind, Body, Soul Journal*, you will see yourself grow into your true, authentic self, living on purpose with intention and unconditional love.

The *Mind, Body, Soul Journal* will prompt you to explore what your true calling is and help you look at life through a new lens so you can express all that you hold within your mind, body and soul to help discover your Divine purpose in life.

Each chapter will help you to reignite your inner light, to transform your life so you are consciously living on purpose. Through a process of introspection and self-discovery you will attract more balance, freedom and fulfilment so you can truly shine and reach your full potential.

The simple practice of writing forces you to reflect on your life, and writing down your thoughts can be a cathartic process that helps you to clarify exactly what it is you want, who you truly are and where it is you are going in life.

Making changes in life is not about one-off actions: it is about forming new habits to transform your life. Start today and discover how to live and how to shape your life with a commanding sense of purpose, divinity and meaning.

Following the simple prompts in this book can help you to discover the happiness that unfolds from realising your full potential. Each section has powerful tools and exercises for unlocking the vast potential of your mind, body and soul to help you achieve your best life imaginable.

'**MEDITATION**
*is the sharp tool to dig out the
great treasure hidden within
everybody's inner personality.*'

– Maharishi Mahesh Yogi

MEDITATION

There is mounting evidence to support the role of the mind in goal setting, healing, sport psychology and living a healthier life. I truly believe everyone can have success with hypnosis and meditation if they can harness the mind, body and spirit connection.

I was fuelled by my faith in myself to heal, my positive expectation that I would have success and my desire to keep going. Like any form of training, it requires commitment – I flexed my mental healing muscles every day until I could really see, and most importantly feel, the benefits! I have now adapted my hypnosis relaxations and use them in all areas of my life and they are the foundation of all the wonderful abundance I experience. As a trained hypnotherapist I have created my own relaxing meditations to accompany each chapter of the journal.

Each specially devised meditation is used as an extra tool to support each month's theme, and if you use them daily, I believe you will achieve great success. They are available on www.andreahayes.ie/media. It is important to commit to the daily practice of checking in with your inner navigation system and subconscious mind – the practice is to believe it, follow its lead and have faith that the upcoming year will be the best of your life. A daily habit of meditation with a focus on mindfulness is essential as you enter a new year because the present moment is always where life is unfolding.

If you are new to this and haven't read *My Life Goals Journal*, you can read full details on how to use the daily audio on my website and also access all the audio links.

'TO BE NOBODY BUT YOURSELF
IN A WORLD WHICH IS DOING
ITS BEST DAY AND NIGHT
TO MAKE YOU LIKE EVERYBODY ELSE
MEANS TO FIGHT THE HARDEST BATTLE
WHICH ANY HUMAN BEING CAN FIGHT
AND NEVER STOP FIGHTING.'

– E. E. Cummings

MONTH 1

Starting Point

'Believe in yourself and all that you are. Know that there is something inside you that is greater than any obstacle.'

– Christian D. Larson

Are you ready to begin your journey? The fact that you found this book is a starting point: imagine this moment as a gateway to something greater. Now is the time to reconnect with what really matters and find out who you truly are. Are you ready to slow down, become aware and sit with the inner stillness of your mind, body and soul so you can truly discover happiness, peace and fulfilment in each moment?

For the next few months, I invite you to begin following your own path to a greater you! Each chapter will act as a guide, while your inner journey will allow you to arrive at the profound realisation that what you seek is already available to you once you connect with your distinctive soul signature. This is your unique essence, your true identity and the foundation of your life mission. Then all the wisdom you require to make life changes and reveal your true purpose will become effortless.

We are all seeking greater meaning. However, we live in a world that largely focuses on the physical side of wellness, which, in this day and age, includes healthy eating, a fit body and how attractive we look. While this is important, it's working from the outside and I feel we need to begin from the inside out.

The busier we become, the harder it is to achieve balance between mental and spiritual wellbeing. I believe a combination of mental, physical and spiritual wellness is undeniably essential to each person in order to find our true, authentic self, a deeper love or that vibrant health and happiness we all crave. As the mind, body and soul are so intrinsically intertwined, I feel it is essential to maintain equilibrium between each to achieve true peace. Learning to honour each part of my being has lead me on a transformational journey of self-discovery and freedom.

Trust me: this is your starting point to finding your true self. Allow yourself to escape while reading the ideas shared here and allow the journal prompts and exercises to guide you as you discover and reconnect with the deepest part of your mind, body and soul – your Divine self.

You will be led to a place where you will experience balance, wellness, spiritual awakening, emotional awareness and greater physical health, vitality and direction in life – the part of you that exists on a higher level: the higher self.

'We do not build or create
A SPIRITUAL
CONSCIOUSNESS;
we merely get rid of all that
OBSCURES OUR
PURE VISION.'

– Roy Davis

I followed my own path to self-discovery and transformation and I believe you can too. If you follow the steps, journaling prompts, exercises and meditations on my website, www.andreahayes.ie/media, you will have the tools to reconnect with the deepest part of yourself and access the profound wisdom within you to help you unlock your potential and create and live the life that is right for you.

It can appear challenging at first, but every challenge in life provides an opportunity to discover a deeper meaning to your life. So even making a decision to live a more balanced life, to find a better path, to get to know what your mind, body and soul are craving for now is a momentous start in itself.

AN 'INSIDE-OUT' PLAN

If you're seeking a more fulfilling way forward, the only place to start is with you. You can't expect great change to manifest from the outside, as it has to happen **within** you.

For years I believed there was some sort of universal power that could shift energy to align events to bring me the outcome I desired, or that certain healers possessed some kind of magic to carry out my decisions, ambitions and goals just the way I wanted. The truth is, there was a way to attract what I wanted in life, and I did discover a magic formula, but to my amazement – the magic was within *me*. It was my commitment to align my energy, values and heartfelt vision of the perfect me that manifested the life I wanted and the person I am today.

Believe in your dream for yourself, but remember that a dream must be envisaged and then built from a solid foundation. The building blocks for your dream are motivation, commitment, persistence, self-discovery and discipline, and, most important, the cement that holds it all together is unconditional love. These are the magic ingredients that have changed my life and I believe they can change your life too.

I am a great believer in setting goals; it has worked for me in the past. I have identified goals I wanted to achieve and I believed they would bring me closer to a more balanced life. But I discovered that when I achieved the goal there was something still lacking inside – I didn't feel fulfilled. However, following the mind, body, soul journaling journey helped me to achieve the bliss and contentment I was craving.

Some people carry a goal with them like a heavy load for years and years – it weighs them down. Often people have a goal they're pursuing, yet years later this goal might remain in the distance. I don't think this is a bad thing – maybe the goal wasn't aligned with their true desire.

Unknowingly, we build our expectations on how we measure up to everyone else. We see people on social media having better lives than us: they seem happier, more successful, fitter, thinner, richer, funnier, more creative and everything about their lives makes us feel worse about ours, but that's where *we* are going wrong! The minute you mark your place in life by measuring it against anyone else, you are engaging in a losing battle.

The first important lesson on this journey is to accept we cannot start a journey of self-discovery and bliss from a place of comparison, hate, negativity and frustration, and expect the outcome to be a life of balance, success, peace and abundance. Believe in yourself and trust in the journaling process.

Accept now: you cannot compare or
contrast yourself to anyone else.

Along the way I will ask you to step out of your comfort zone to do some of the work needed for transformation. These will be the dares of the day, week and month.

Go on, dare yourself to do the work
so you can truly follow your heart's desire.

DARE OF THE DAY

Today I want you to ask your heart this one question:
What is your true desire?

Answer the question in your personal journal or above and see what comes up for you. It might only be a few words or it could be a complete plan, but just ask yourself what you desire right now. And allow this question to stay with you for the whole day.

You might find it hard to answer that question and that's OK – don't put any pressure on yourself. Simply reflect on the question over the course of the day.

'SOMETIMES IT'S
THE JOURNEY THAT
TEACHES YOU A LOT
ABOUT YOUR
DESTINATION.'

– Drake

Sometimes it is difficult to get started when you are not in the habit of writing so below are some questions that you can use as prompts to get you started.

DARE OF THE WEEK

During this week, take time to journal. Pick a few of the questions below – the ones that resonate the most with you – and get started. If you're a journaling beginner, or you're not sure about all of this, I suggest you take 15 minutes and do one. If you have time, or want to challenge yourself more, take an hour and write on two or more of these prompts. You might want to do this in your personal journal or on the blank pages at the end of this chapter.

These questions are designed to help you clarify your perspective, not mentally torture yourself. If it feels awkward, stop. But importantly, be honest. If you have made this commitment to write, then do your best to write honestly – there is no point in lying to yourself. Remember, you can choose to burn your journal later if you have to: just get it out, onto the page – think of it as free therapy.

WHO ARE YOU?

Think of your core values, the repeated behaviours that make up your day, your passions, dislikes, predominant thoughts – what parts make up the sum of your life?

WHAT DO YOU WANT?

If you didn't have to worry about money or people's opinions, what would you do with your life?

WHAT DO YOU KNOW FOR SURE? *OR* WHAT DO YOU WANT TO KNOW?

Look at your life experience, the lessons learned, the talents and abilities you are confident in. Think of what your heart feels touched by or softened towards learning more about. What makes your mind curious?

WHAT IS YOUR UNIQUE PURPOSE OR CALLING IN LIFE?

Review your life: what do you like doing? Think about what you think you should or should not do – why do you feel that way?

'Trust is like the air we breathe. WHEN IT'S PRESENT, NOBODY REALLY NOTICES. But when it's absent, everybody notices.'

– Warren Buffett

DARE OF THE MONTH

For this month, try to examine the following seven positive steps that will point you in the right direction on your mind, body, soul journey. I suggest choosing one step and working on the theme of that step in your journal for a few days and over this month you should aim to complete all seven steps. You can opt to continue for a little longer on the theme in your own separate journal, or skip a step below and come back to it to review at the end of the month.

STEP 1 – LET GO OF COMPARISONS

This is your first step to a new awareness of self. Measuring our physical appearance, material possessions, personal life, romantic relationships, career and so on against anyone else is toxic, deflating and a hazardous habit you need to stop today. Making this little internal decision not to worry about anyone else's life or what they think of you is a small step that is enough to propel you in the right direction.

I always say, what people think of me is their business – just acknowledging that and honouring the meaning suddenly after years of feeling stuck, I felt free to move, spread my wings and go after what I wanted. I had nothing to lose and needed no one's approval.

It is important, too, to remember there is more to life than your achievements so don't allow your inner critic to tell you that you haven't achieved or done enough. If we listen to that voice we are feeding our self-judgement.

This new habit of celebrating our unique self takes daily practice and awareness. So how do you break out of the destructive comparison cycle? For me, the first thing was to let go of my preconceived ideas about where I thought I would be by the time I reached my current age. When I looked at the time I spent measuring myself against others, I suddenly realised it was the biggest time thief in my life, and the place where most of the crime was being committed was on social media. This modern cyberspace has made it perfectly acceptable and easy to engage in the sort of behaviour we would have called stalking a few years ago!

This digital age is entirely dedicated to making you lust after things you don't have – we are bombarded with picture-perfect images of flawlessness. Think about it: if you spend a few hours every day being force-fed these images, you will be literally bloated with feelings of inadequacy, envy and sometimes even self-hate.

It is OK to admire someone else or value them for inspiration, but the only person to compare yourself to is the person you were yesterday.

I celebrate my unique self by:

....

....

STEP 2 – UNPLUG

Stop with social media – call it a digital detox or an un-follow Friday or just unplug from the constant distraction and start to follow your own heart. If you are not on social media, maybe you need to **stop** the internal dialogue of where you feel you **should** be in life right now. Whatever it is that is swallowing your time and holding you back, it is time to unplug and start afresh. Dig deep and detach yourself from distraction or comparison to others and realise today can be your new beginning.

Maybe you may have spent years trying to be or do what the world wants from you, rather than what you want from it. Trying to be someone else or another version of yourself can leave you in a constant state of unease, always questioning everything you have or haven't achieved, asking yourself is it enough? Am I enough?

Acknowledge right now you are perfect just the way you are right now. Every day your job is to seek out that picture of perfection of yourself and enhance it and let it grow.

I am enough because:

....

....

STEP 3 - CLEAR A SPACE: MAKE TIME FOR YOU!

They say that one of the best things you can give yourself is time – time to open up and know yourself more. I know that can be an overwhelming idea. Ignorance of my true self or what I truly wanted is something I lived with for a long time.

Self-discovery means many things. It means finding your purpose in life (we all have a purpose). It means digging deep into your childhood and revealing the experiences that shaped you (both good and bad). It means realising what your core values and beliefs are and living by them.

Having a greater sense of who you are can propel you towards achieving your boundless potential. And creating time and space to do more of what drives you is a good place to begin, but it often isn't that simple. First you need to learn what you are passionate about. To discover what that is for you, I will ask you to take some time out to be silent and try to find a mindful moment.

I made it my intention to go on this self-discovery journey and prioritised time for myself to just be tranquil. Starting off, you should ideally take at least 15 minutes a day to just sit and be silent, without a TV, radio, phone or people as a distraction. After time you will increase this and you might even choose to go on a silent weekend retreat to explore how powerful the act of silence truly is. Many of my biggest insights happened during my mindful moments of stillness.

My mindful moment today revealed:

....

....

STEP 4 - FIND YOUR PURPOSE

When we do anything, we always do it with purpose – even if that purpose is not immediately obvious to anyone else, even the individual involved. This is true of plants and animals, and it is certainly true of human beings. All movement is to achieve purpose. And you may ask yourself, 'What is my conscious purpose in life?'

ASKING

* Take a moment just to relax.

* Pay attention inwardly as you close your eyes.

* Focus on just your breath for a minute.

* Now see what comes to mind when you ask **'What is my conscious purpose in life?'**

RECEIVING

* Let the answer come.

* Receive whatever comes in an open, non-judgemental way.

* Stay with it a while, even if it is only a slight insight or it might be nothing.

* Journal your answer to see what this starting point is for you.

This is the beginning of allowing your mind, body and soul to direct you towards the larger creative role you need to play in the world.

Remember, our consciousness is part of something much bigger: it is part of the planet's consciousness, part of the solar system's consciousness, part of the universal consciousness, the cosmic consciousness. When you become aware of your oneness with this consciousness at a mind-body-soul level, much vaster wisdom than you presently possess can become available to you in meditation.

What is my conscious purpose in life?

_____

_____

STEP 5 – CHALLENGE YOUR IDEA OF SUCCESS

We live in a world where everyone is looking, aiming and wanting to be at that elusive finishing line of success. But what is success?

Life is not a race: you don't have just one opportunity to carry out your vision or achieve a goal. If you failed to carry it out in the past, that's OK – you don't need to wait for the beginning of next year. Open that new page in your story and start now: see this moment as the beginning of the new, better and happier you.

You can make a new resolution every day, and you can start again every day if you fail – see it as an opportunity to learn, to grow and to do better. In fact, I removed failure from my lexicon when I approached my new beginning, and it took away any fear I had attached to not achieving what I set out to do. I replaced fear with feelings of happiness and with the anticipation that great and wonderful things are going to manifest for me at the perfect time – I would be the measure of my own success.

Don't allow any external yardstick to become the measure of *your* success.

I am a success today because:

....

....

....

....

STEP 6 – START A NEW CHAPTER TODAY

Let's begin your story now. All writers and storytellers start with plotlines, characters and conversations, but they also need the Big Idea to make the reader turn the page. How can you make your life a page-turner? What storyline would excite you right now? If you could write the perfect plot for your life, what dream sees you racing to grab a pen and paper and jot it down before it slips away?

Questions are great because they really make your brain work and they can offer great insight on your journey.

Below are what I call **soul questions** – you will see them throughout this journal. Try to fill in what comes to mind below, which will shape the plot of this new chapter in your life story.

What better way is seeking you?

_____

_____

_____

What do you want from life?

_____

_____

_____

How do you see yourself living in five years' time or ten years' time?

_____

_____

_____

What is your heart yearning for?

_____

_____

_____

What is your true calling in this life?

_____

_____

_____

What ignites your life?

_____

_____

_____

'Your health is your starting point – without it, you have nothing.'

– Sienna Guillory

Another question you might want to explore this month in your own personal journal is the story of you! It might be helpful to ask yourself what has brought you to this point right now. Look at all the areas of your life (family, home, leisure, career, finance, health and so on) and see what feels out of balance. When you evaluate these areas against your long-term vision for your life story, are you going in the right direction? How can you bring yourself closer to that vision? Are some things in your life more of a distraction or burden?

Every story has a starting point, and for me it was my health.

In 2012, after a diagnosis of Chiari malformation, I decided to take what was to be three months off work. This ended up being a changing point in my life. I chose *me* instead of work and something shifted. I started on this journey of learning who my true, authentic self was.

Now I have come further than I could see back then, when I started walking that path in Marlay Park, looking for answers and trusting myself to know the right way forward. If I look at where I started from and where I have reached, I have a sense of achievement that is very personal to me.

That's the important message: your beginning is just yours alone; it's unique to you. It is important to value and appreciate your own story and your starting point. While the achievements and benchmarks will change, and your goals might evolve with time, your starting point will not. The heart is the true seat of power, so we need to begin with love, unconditional love for this special journey, and allow it to unfold gracefully, in its own time.

You need to begin at this starting point with patience, love, perseverance and a deep trust that all will work out fine, as you are allowing yourself to be guided by the Divine wisdom within you, your own precious navigation system that knows what your mind, body and soul truly desires.

A great sense of accomplishment and success comes from doing what you love or doing something that has great meaning for your true self. When you listen to the calling of your heart, you engage in work that has real meaning and lasting value. You are filled with a strong sense of fulfilment as you connect to the true nature of what you are destined to do.

Self-discovery should be an important goal for everyone. Some people go through life playing a role and masking who they really are. If you're not sure how to set about probing your psyche and emotional depths, the journaling prompts could help you to embark on your journey of self-discovery and write your story.

This is work only you can do – adjustments will be needed; maybe a new purpose or direction will need to be discovered. Don't try to force it: just follow your own path and the chapters ahead at your own pace. Write your own story from this starting point in your own separate writing place if you want to really explore your life path so far. When I did this for the first time, little did I know that what I was writing would form the seeds of my first book, *Pain-free Life: My Journey to Wellness*.

The writing journey, however, will not always be an easy one. It may include fear, confusion, misunderstanding, doubt and revisiting all your choices in life. I like to refer to it as decluttering your mind, spring-cleaning your soul and recharging your body. It may require making some tough decisions and sticking to them, which means change (including the places, situations and people in your life). My journey so far has seen me detach from situations and cut people from my life that weren't serving my greater good.

Make it your intention to enjoy the deep, profound, positive transformation. Like winter, it can feel like a cold, barren place to start, where nothing is visible and no signs of growth can be seen, but once you commit to taking the journey with courage, strength and patience, you can trust that things are happening beneath the surface. The promise of spring will soon be visible.

Express your feelings along the way in your journal in a loving, gentle and honest way, without judgement. Let yourself be vulnerable and know that you are coming from a place of unconditional love; love is the starting point for all ways forward. If you start each entry from a place of love, I promise there will be peace and harmony in your everyday experiences, for everything becomes a reflection of how you feel truly on the inside.

Your positive, empowering thoughts will inspire your actions, and your new actions can change your circumstances. So to change your life you must change your thinking and become the master of your mind.

I understand that at times it can be easier to settle for the status quo – staying in a job for monetary reasons, remaining in a toxic relationship because you don't want to be alone, not speaking your truth with family and friends or living in a negative space because it is easier than shifting the state of affairs – but if you are brave enough to honour your truth and change your direction, this action could trigger a massive shift in your life that will be the catalyst for you living a life of purpose, happiness and abundance.

So take time to truly reflect on what really matters to you now. Can you define where you are at this time in your life and do you know what new direction you want to go in?

WRITE YOUR STORY:

'HAPPINESS RADIATES like the fragrance from a flower, and DRAWS ALL GOOD things toward you.'

– Maharishi Mahesh Yogi

MONTHLY REVIEW

JOURNAL WORK

Take time to write each day and get into the habit of sharing your thoughts and ideas on the pages of your journal. You can use the blank pages at the end of this chapter or your own separate writing space. You can choose to write about what you want, write about the insights you have had so far or revisit some of the themes you read about this month. The important thing is to keep writing.

Choose a journaling prompt from the list below to work on and you should soon begin to see a clear direction.

* Write about something you learned from forgiveness.

* Write about something you learned from fear.

* Write about something you learned from contentment.

* Write about something you learned from love.

* Write about something you learned from joy.

MEDITATION

This month we begin our path to finding the true authentic you with a relaxation. You will find this first month is all about creating positive change and embracing your starting point on this transformational journey. The meditation will also have suggestions to encourage daily journaling so it will help you begin your new habit of writing daily. Try to listen to it as often as you can to get the best benefits. You will find it at Month 1 of my Mind, Body, Soul Journal audio space on my website, www.andreahayes.ie.

My Journal Extract

I am journaling about going through some dark times in my life. This isn't something I like to do, as I would rather not revisit some parts of my past, but I feel I need to go through the darkness in order to really see clearly. We need to reveal the shadows just as much as the light. Going through this darkness is scary – I know I am going to uncover the hurts of my past, and already I feel fearful, isolated, worried and lonely again. I experienced a lot of loneliness as a child and it resurfaces easily as I write and think about my past.

When I bring myself back to those dark moments and allow myself to sit with those feelings again, nothing seems to fit or make sense. While I was meditating on some questions like 'What are my past hurts?' I felt I was in a kind of smoke-filled place: it was hard to see ahead and also hard to breathe. In that darkness, I didn't seem to know which was up or down. One thing I did feel in the darkness was that I was 'held' by something bigger and stronger than myself, and somehow this made me feel safer. I needed to surrender to the feelings. They have scorched my soul and I know it is time to heal. I need to forgive the past hurts in order to break through into the light.

As I sat in silence, I had a conversation with God and asked for his forgiveness for my part in my past hurts and it was a very powerful feeling. I sat with that feeling of forgiveness and I was surprised by what and who came to mind. Then I said sorry to those people and sent them love and peace.

I am not sure how long I stayed in this space but I felt something shifted in me. I feel even lighter writing about this.

I forgive you, Andrea.

I thank you, Andrea.

And I love you, Andrea.

A x

My Journal

'Though no one can go back and make a brand new start, anyone can start from now and make a brand new ending.'

– Carl Bard

'SELF-APPROVAL AND SELF-ACCEPTANCE in the now are the main keys to POSITIVE CHANGES in every area of our lives.'

– Louise L. Hay

MONTH 2

The Path to Unconditional Self-Acceptance

'When you arise in the morning, think of what a **PRECIOUS PRIVILEGE** it is to be alive –

TO BREATHE, TO THINK, TO ENJOY, TO LOVE.'

– Marcus Aurelius

I made it my intention to live in bliss, and I focused on what that would mean for me. This extended period of self-discovery and self-reflection led me to a huge life-changing realisation. It is all about unconditional love.

When we think of unconditional love, the first thing we might think of is the love a parent has for a child. But many of us do not strive to have those same feelings for ourselves. As a mother, I absolutely love, adore and cherish my children, in spite of their imperfections and mistakes, and this love is unquestioned. I can never, ever imagine feeling any emotion other than pure love for my daughters. This love will never need to be earned or measured.

Looking into the eyes of a newborn baby we see perfection. We love our children without reservation – when we love completely, we accept them just how they are, as perfect little beings. It is a love that knows no boundaries.

So why do we not have that love without reservation for ourselves?

Maybe we could say that not everyone receives unconditional love from their parents. I was fortunate enough that my life was graced by someone whom I will always consider the great love of my life, my mother. Her love could reach beyond any worldly boundary.

Simply put, her unconditional love was her unlimited, loving way of seeing me. I was without any limit in her thoughts and feelings about my life. I felt her love. The faith she had in me created a reality where anything was possible for me. As a child, despite severe hearing problems and other medical setbacks, she made me believe I could achieve anything. I couldn't read or write until I was almost eight years of age, yet I didn't once feel that I didn't measure up to others. I was developing perfectly in my mother's eyes and I felt totally loved just the way I was. Her love was so natural and pure – it came straight from the wellspring of her heart. With it, I could truly flourish, prosper and develop my full potential as her child.

But somewhere along the way from childhood to becoming an adult, I started to erode my own unconditional love for myself. I started to love with condition, a self-love with limits. Those limiting beliefs started to creep in. Negative, judgemental thoughts encouraged my inner critic to grow into an inner judge and jury who served to make me feel guilty. In many ways, we sentence ourselves to a life of disappointment, failure, self-loathing, anger and frustration by feeding that inner voice of self-hatred.

True self-love is freedom from the shackles that hold us back and make us believe we are not enough.

End your prison sentence today. Allow love to be the prevailing feeling you have about life. I work with animals and I have witnessed how they truly love unconditionally. They allow the highest levels of love in their awareness to permeate every experience they have with their master. Think about it: a dog will always greet you warmly if you're the master, and when you operate in this space of love, you are literally vibrating to a higher frequency of energy. You cannot but feel loved when your dog wags its tail to meet you after a busy day, and allowing that energy to move forth into your world truly lifts your spirit and your vibration.

So to start our journey we need to make a conscious decision to begin with a sense of **pure love** in all our thoughts and feelings. Think of your soul's journey as an evolving process of development. Make it your loving intention to allow your soul to grow in consciousness, steadily progressing through different levels and stages of awareness.

It will be different for everyone, so you need to explore your own ideas about what unconditional love means to you.

'The only way
**LOVE CAN LAST
A LIFETIME**
is if it is
UNCONDITIONAL.'

– Stephen Kendrick

DARE OF THE DAY

Choose five things you love about yourself and write them all down.

1. ....

2. ....

3. ....

4. ....

5. ....

Then ask yourself: what does unconditional love mean to me?

For me **love** is an expression of life, a sense of personal peace, pure bliss and the most powerful emotion a human can experience. It represents all the virtues I want to embody: kindness, compassion, empathy, caring and understanding. Love trusts, love is patient and love does not judge or hate. When we love, we are in a state of grace, there is no panic, fear or uncertainty. Similarly, we do not see fault, blame or shame. The language of love isn't aggressive or controlling. When we come from a place of love we don't manipulate, criticise, judge, compare or condemn. It is the one infinite emotion that has the power to change our own world and the world around us.

Now that we have defined some aspects of love, let us turn to our attention to the other word: **unconditional.** To be unconditional is to be without condition or limit. When something is unlimited, it has no boundaries, no measure. Something that is unfailing and everlasting. It means no strings attached, no stipulations and no expectations.

You must love yourself before you
can truly love anyone else.

This well-known truism makes perfect sense: we can't really know love until we experience it from within – for ourselves. This was a massive struggle for me, as I didn't feel I loved myself fully and without conditions.

If you were to be totally honest, would you say that you really and truly love yourself right now?

The foundation for a positive sense of self is complete acceptance. You need to love yourself in the present moment as you are, not as you may be. This doesn't mean that you should never change, but that you're able to live with who you are in your own skin right now without criticism. I think today, more than ever, people are constantly revamping themselves and performing makeovers, not just on their appearance or home but on their personality, life and even their abilities. We never seem to be happy. Sometimes this unease with oneself and lack of self-love and self-acceptance can stem back to childhood. American psychologist Carl Rogers wrote about this at great length. According to Rogers, when parents place 'conditions of worth' on young children, they cause their offspring to grow up to be self-doubters and critics. This is when the self-critic is born: we develop an inner voice that constantly compares the actual self to how we feel we 'should' be. Personally, I replaced the word 'should' with 'could', which takes off any pressure of feeling that I *have to* do something. Using the word 'could' means I have a choice to do it – and choice brings freedom.

So to begin on a path of self-love, you need to remember to listen to your own self-talk, identify the thoughts, attitudes or behaviours behind it, explore where these beliefs stemmed from and ask yourself if they are getting in the way of accepting yourself without measure right now.

DARE OF THE WEEK

This week, try making a conscious effort to do something each day that scares you. Explore the true essence of *you* by facing your fears. It could be you ask for more money at work, you reach out to an old friend, you might join a gym or start something new!

To adopt the bravery you need to try something new in your life, start each day with the powerful **I am** exercise. Simply use the words 'I am' before the quality you want to feel for the day, then repeat it to yourself several times. For example, 'I am successful, I am successful, I am successful,' allows a more personal and direct connection to the power held within the quality of success. It seems simplistic, but repeating the **I am** mantra will cause a change in your perspective and how you experience life, so be prepared to become a new you.

Become a self-lover rather than a self-critic

Some qualities of **I am** you might want to attract are on the opposite page. Decide which quality you want and use it as a daily mantra or affirmation: repeat it, write it down and embrace it. For example: I am kind. Today I embraced this by donating some clothes to charity.

Try doing this each day for a week and see how your energy shifts.

Affectionate WISE

Artistic INVENTIVE

SEXY *AMBITIOUS* Charismatic

KIND Exuberant

JOYFUL *Courageous*

Compassionate Wealthy

Empathetic

Intuitive FUN

BRAVE *Passionate*

I am:

....

Today I embraced this by:

....

I am:

....

Today I embraced this by:

....

I am:

....

Today I embraced this by:

....

I am:

....

Today I embraced this by:

....

I am:

....

Today I embraced this by:

....

I am:

....

Today I embraced this by:

....

DARE OF THE MONTH

Let's examine **four positive ways** you can begin on the road to a life-long loving relationship with the self. I suggest choosing one of the themes below and working on it for a week – you will soon start to see the breakthroughs.

WEEK 1: EGO

When you make it your intention to truly love yourself, you need to have **ego awareness**. The personality or ego tries to make the process of self-love complicated, so you need to learn to identify ego thoughts and transcend them. This would be a lot easier if we knew what the ego was exactly. Some say the ego is just an illusion. I have also heard it described as '**E**dging **G**od **O**ut', and that's what it means to me.

Consider the following analogy. An actor plays a part when he is on stage; he plays it so well many applaud him for his performance and believe his character to be true. If when he leaves the stage he remains forever in character, he isn't being his true self – he is just following the plot of someone else's play.

When we start to live our lives according to a script that we believe to be true for us, it is a false identity that we are acting out: this is the ego taking centre stage in our life. We are putting on a show, a mask and a performance, and forgetting to be our true self.

> Ego: a person's sense of self-esteem or self-importance.
> The part of the mind that mediates between the
> conscious and the unconscious and is responsible for
> reality testing and a sense of personal identity.

So how do you unmask the ego identity? Remember, the ego character is part of a script we have constructed: it is a false identity we devised to play a part. It is often built from beliefs about what we *think* we are – beliefs about our personality, talents and abilities. Our true personality is made up of our ego personality and our authentic personality: who we are when we play the part and who we are when we come off stage. The kinds of thoughts that contribute to the ego personality are:

'I'm not good at singing.'
'I am a great salesperson.'
'My hips make me ugly.'
'Nobody likes me.'
'I am the best person at the job.'
'I am stupid for trusting him.'

When we have thoughts about **I** or **me** that we agree with, we construct a self-image. Watch out for what is attached to **I** and **me** when you're making declarative statements as above, as it could be the ego and not the true reality of your self. We need to always ask ourselves if these statements are actual truths or only part of a script our egos have constructed to play a part.

The ego is attached to things, titles and possessions: these are the props needed for the performance. As soon as you lose one or all of them, the ego loses its sense of identity and gets stage fright. When this happens in your life, you might lose your confidence – as the attachments of ego fall away so too does your self-worth.

Working on the ego is an **inside job**: it is all about uncovering the true self, our authentic personality. To do this, we must learn to stop acting out parts and surrender the script and props so we can walk offstage and become our true selves.

Loving ourselves begins with accepting ourselves right *now*. The play we invented, the actor we became and the props we think we need are just subconscious manifestations of a past thought or feeling we held about our self that we wrote into a script.

1. You are not your job.
2. You are not your material possessions.
3. You are not your achievements.
4. You are not your weight.
5. You are not your mistakes.
6. You are not your family.
7. You are not a title like mother, husband, parent.

Don't allow your identity to be wrapped up in the limiting thoughts or attachments of your ego.

You are not your ego attachments or props.

For me, the ego becomes extremely obvious when I am criticised. I go back to a childhood place of judgement; I feel I am not enough; it hurts me to be judged so I play the part of being strong and defensive. I project my past hurt into the present situation and often over-compensate with achievements. I am aware of this now and work hard to identify it, understand it and detach from it.

What offends or hurts you can often be trying to teach you a lesson. So watch your mind – this is when the ego starts to reveal itself.

Our ego lives in the part of our mind that's impulsive rather than logical, often stirring reactions buried deep in the subconscious mind. Often when we have inner judgement or a mental argument with ourselves, we're having a conflict with our ego.

Be aware: the next time you face criticism, rather than reacting to it, let it be an opportunity to show grace and learn what it can reveal. One of Eckhart Tolle's most helpful exercises is to occasionally allow the diminishment of your ego. When someone criticises you, don't immediately retaliate or condemn the other person. Allow the ego to die a little bit.

Surrender your need for control: accept that you are not your ego, which means you are not the actor in the script you may have been following, and you don't need the props you think you need to form your character. So accept you are not your title, your job, your accomplishments or your material possessions – try to let go of these attachments.

Break free of playing the character and move away from the stage and the desire to perform and be applauded for your actions. Use the space below or explore in your personal writing space what it might mean to you to take risks and do what makes you happy.

I choose to release my ego attachments by:

'The weak can never forgive. **FORGIVENESS IS THE ATTRIBUTE OF THE STRONG.**'

– Mahatma Gandhi

One of the most empowering things we can do is harness the **art of forgiveness**. I have read that forgiveness is the 'exquisite healer' in all of us. Forgiveness will open the windows to your soul – it is the key to releasing any emotional baggage we continue to carry. Remember, everything has an expiration date so don't be afraid to let go of your out-dated perspectives on yourself or any other attachment that keeps you bound to your past.

The mistakes and failures of the past are gone; we must move on and see them as an opportunity to grow and learn. Think of the old saying, **'You live and you learn'**. Release your past hurts, mistakes and traumas. Forgive yourself and stop holding a space in your heart for the pain – let it go with love.

> Note to self: no situation in life
> is beyond the act of forgiveness.

When we live in a constant state of blame and resentment we are carrying a heavy load that weighs the spirit and stops it from soaring. I was surprised to discover I had baggage hidden deep within, past hurts I was still carrying. I was angry at my parents; I was still incredibly pissed off at a friend who I felt had 'done me wrong'; some of the things I did in my past brought up feelings of embarrassment and shame – unconsciously and unaware, I carried all of those emotions around with me every day!

I found a very easy exercise that helped me to release those attachments and allowed me to move on and forgive. It's so simple, yet the outcome was profound – it's hard to articulate how much it has changed my life.

This one mantra can set you free:

I forgive you.
I send you love.
Thank you.

This week, try this forgiveness exercise.

Close your eyes, sit quietly and peacefully allow your mind to think of the people who are hardest to forgive.

In your journal, make a physical list of every single thing that has been done to you that you can't forgive – people, situations or incidents that you are holding onto and that have played on your mind for years.

* every relationship problem you've had,

* teachers who embarrassed you,

* family members who hurt you,

* friends who were nasty or bitchy to you,

* an ex-lover who broke your heart,

* bosses who criticised you, made you feel bad or made you cry,

* strangers who made you feel bad by making comments,

* somebody who broke your trust.

Write it all down.

Now, look back at your list and for each person or situation decide:

The person I need to forgive is ....

and I forgive you for ....

Mentally affirm to that person or situation:

I forgive you.
I send you love.
And thank you.

Spend a couple of seconds on each one and then move on. Don't get caught up in the emotion. You are only saying the mantra and releasing the memory. You may feel an overwhelming outpouring of sadness, anger or other emotions but just continue the mantra.

* *I forgive you* evaporates the energy of resentment you hold towards them.
* *I send you love* balances the energy, sends love to the situation and releases you from being the victim.
* *Thank you* wraps everything with gratitude, which heals old wounds and changes the energy.

Then try to turn your attention to yourself. Think about and list the things you've done that you feel bad about. Here are some examples to get you started:

Something really important that you failed at:

....

....

Something you did in school that still haunts you:

....

....

A bad decision or judgement:

....

....

Dumping someone in a really horrible way:

....

....

Gossiping behind someone's back:

....

....

Making someone cry (intentionally or not):

....

....

Stealing something – no matter how small:

....

....

Cheating:

....

....

Letting someone down:

....

....

Telling lies:

....

....

Then for each item you have written down, say out loud:
'I forgive myself for ....'

Try using forgiveness in other areas of your life and see if it makes a difference. It is a mental shift in how you view your world; you are switching your lens.

* Forgive money for abandoning you.

* Forgive your bank for raising interest rates.

* Forgive your thighs and bum for holding onto fat.

* Forgive your car for breaking down.

* Forgive the government for its failings.

These forgiveness rituals might seem unusual, but try them – things will start to shift in your subconscious and in how you view the world. They may cause some past emotions to bubble to the surface, but afterwards you will feel lighter and better for it. Don't be surprised if something changes with a person or situation that you have forgiven!

'LOVE YOURSELF.
Forgive yourself.
BE TRUE TO YOURSELF.
How you treat yourself
sets the standard for how
others will treat you.'

– Steve Maraboli

Over the years I have been a big fan of the late, great Louise L. Hay. She has written many books on healing and self-love and these have had a huge impact on many people because they provide some effective techniques to help you begin to love yourself. She was a great believer in the power of affirmations, which train your mind to focus on the positive instead of the negative.

A few years ago, when I was beginning my journey, I took a large piece of paper and wrote out powerful self-love affirmations and stuck them to the side of a mirror in my bedroom. Each time I looked in the mirror I repeated them with feeling. I also wrote some on Post-it notes and stuck them around the house and in the car and tried to bring them with me so I could read them easily and freely every day.

Here are seven affirmations that might resonate with you. Choose one for each day this week or make up your own.

1. I love myself unconditionally.
2. I am proud of myself and all that I have accomplished.
3. I respect myself and treat myself with kindness.
4. I let go of all reasons and excuses for not loving myself.
5. I am worthy.
6. I am my own best friend.
7. Self-care comes naturally to me every day.

You could also try looking at yourself in the mirror and telling yourself that you love yourself unconditionally. This might seem a little difficult at first, but it is something that Louise L. Hay endorses and it has worked for me. You can try writing it out below before saying it aloud. Look straight at yourself in the mirror, say 'I love you', followed by your own name and then say things that you love and admire about yourself. You might tell yourself you love yourself because you are a great parent, you are a loyal friend, you are trustworthy, you are hardworking, you are kind, you are generous, you are funny, you are unique, you are loving. Finish again by saying your name and repeating: 'I love you, I really love you'.

Try it for yourself. While looking at yourself in the mirror, say:

I love you, (your name) _____
I love you because _____
I love you, (your name) _____
I really love you, (your name) _____ .

I have done this simple exercise many times over the years. However, when I revisited this exercise with a new appreciation of unconditional love for myself, it had a bigger impact. So, remember, no judgement, no comparisons and saying 'I love you' without limit or measure will have a magnified effect.

It might surprise you to find out how you feel about the person looking back at you in the mirror. Ask yourself:

What do you see when you look in the mirror?

_____

_____

_____

_____

If you commit to addressing anything that comes up when you do this in your journaling work, you might notice areas you need to work on. The final goal here is unconditional self-acceptance and self-love.

When we truly love ourselves, everyone around us benefits – we experience a profound sense of freedom and inner peace. We are able to tune into our true personality and wisdom, and we act upon our highest aspirations from a place of love, not judgement or limitation.

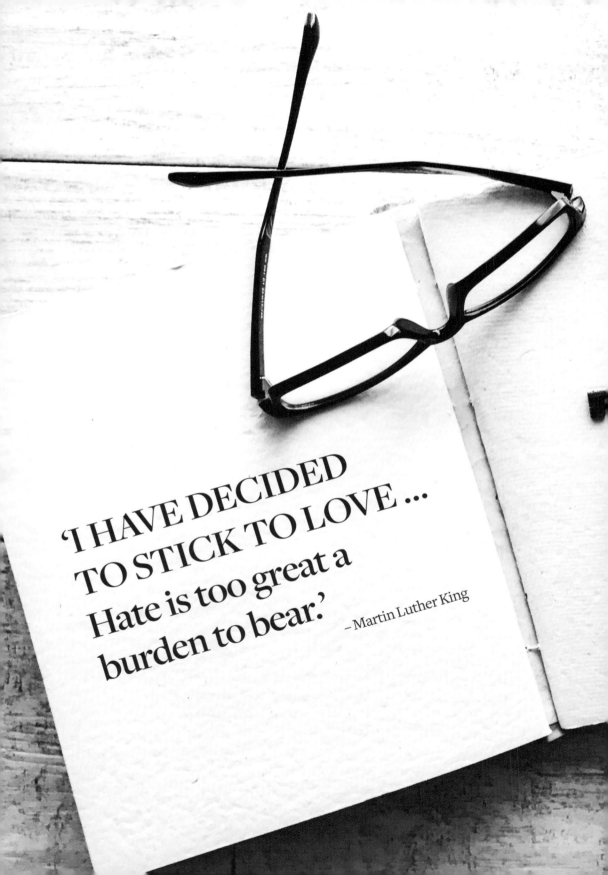

'I HAVE DECIDED TO STICK TO LOVE ... Hate is too great a burden to bear.'

– Martin Luther King

WEEK 4: CONTRACT OF COMMITMENT TO SELF-LOVE

Hopefully by now you will be starting to see yourself in a new light. Loving yourself unconditionally is a continuous process, not a goal. Begin each day with the intention to love yourself – every day we can find greater ways to do this.

Start by affirming that you are doing the very best you can for today. When we remember that each of us does the very best we can at any particular moment, we are well on our way to moving into a space of unconditional love. Love for yourself is the most important love you can feel. We have often heard the statement: 'Love makes the world go round'. I believe this to be true. Love is the binding agent that holds the whole universe together.

Learning to love yourself without limit can be very powerful: suddenly you will have the strength and courage to try new things, to stand up for your true self and to go after your dreams; you will begin to live on purpose because you have that inner knowledge that, no matter what the outcome, you will still love and accept yourself regardless of any actions you take. This insurance can manifest great change.

No one can do it for you. Unconditionally loving the self is a personal commitment and a life-long journey.

Think of when we get married: we are vowing a lifelong devotion to support someone in reaching their highest potential, achieving their dreams and what is important to them in their life. We agree to help them to be as happy as they possibly can, to support them and try to ensure that all of their needs are met.

> Make a love commitment to yourself
> every day to do just that.

Instead of setting big goals for myself I wanted to explore the notion of creating daily contracts with myself. Making a daily commitment to do something small can have a big effect over time, and great changes can be achieved without feeling that the effort has been a burden or a difficult, long process.

The idea of a contract resonates with me: when I take on a job or a new role, I absolutely apply myself without question, 100 per cent. I am known to be a little reluctant to sign contracts, but when I do, I am fully focused and completely committed. How could I apply that same commitment to my everyday life so I could be the best version of myself?

I read about daily contracts in a book by Rick Pitino called *One Day Contract*. I explored the concept of signing a daily agreement with myself to help me incorporate habits or actions that I would focus on just for that day to help me love myself more fully every day.

It was important for me that it was a short-term contract – this made it more achievable and something I could commit to. The other advantage of a one-day self-contract is that if it doesn't work you don't have to continue it, but there is a sense of achievement in completing that day.

The whole purpose of the one-day contract is to add value to your life each day – it shouldn't be something you dread or can't commit to. The benefits can be substantial. When you truly begin to focus all of your energy and effort into making this day the best it can be, you will value the joy in every moment.

Create a binding agreement with yourself, just for today.

Here is an example of one of my contracts. You can create your own with meaning and intention.

13 April

I, Andrea Hayes, agree to the terms of this contract just for today. My intention today is to love myself unconditionally by doing the following:

I will give unconditional love and respect to everyone I encounter.

My time will be spent wisely while directing all of my focus and energy on living with an outlook of love and perfection in all my daily tasks.

Everything that is placed on my 'things to do' list for today will be done lovingly, passionately, easily and effortlessly.

I will learn something new and grow in awareness and love.

I will look at the world around me through the lens of love.

Andrea x

YOUR CONTRACT

__ / __ / __

I, ..., *agree to the terms of this contract just for today.*
My intention today is to love myself unconditionally by doing the following:

....

....

....

....

....

....

....

....

....

....

....

....

Signed: ....

'ACCEPT YOURSELF,
love yourself and
KEEP MOVING FORWARD.
If you want to fly,
you have to give up
what weighs you down.'

– Roy T. Bennett

MONTHLY REVIEW

JOURNAL WORK

Write about what you have learned this month; a word or sentence is enough – you can use your personal writing space or the pages at the end of this chapter to write about it in more detail. Here are some **soul questions** to begin with.

What have you learned about ego attachments and the part they might be playing in your life?

....

....

Is there anything you learned about forgiveness?

....

....

Do you truly love yourself, and why?

....

....

How can you become 1 per cent better today than you were yesterday?

....

....

MEDITATION

If you are new to meditation, you will love this month's meditation, as it is a wonderful tool for quieting the ego and tuning in to the essence of your true self, which is the essence of your creative force. You will find it at Month 2 of my Mind, Body, Soul Journal *audio space on my website, www.andreahayes.ie. If you do not feel the connection right away, keep at it. Listen to the meditation each day this week or for the amount of time needed until you feel you have stopped playing a part in your life and have embraced your true self. Can you say 'I love myself unconditionally' and really mean it?*

My Journal Extract

This week has been really good. I am currently working for myself. I made a contract for myself this morning, stating:

> I, Andrea Hayes, am entering into a loving contract
> with myself for the week ahead.

The plan is to make a new contract each day with a different intention for the day ahead. My intention today is to love myself unconditionally. I did a really powerful meditation and visualisation on unconditional love.

I imagined my mother holding me as a baby – I could see her with a big smile, gently holding me and telling me, 'I'm so glad you were born.' She told me over and over that I am loved, I am perfect, I am safe, I am secure, I am enough.

I let those feelings just settle into my psyche and I felt very emotional and yet very peaceful.

The whole idea of being unconditionally loved has taken on a whole new meaning while I am working on my journey to happiness. I am finding it really powerful. I notice I am breaking the habit of judgement and self-criticism, and I notice the more I am aware of it, the more I seem to be able to go beyond the need to put myself down or think of myself in a negative way. I feel a new energy around me – maybe it's an appreciation of a new vision of myself. It is too early to tell what this new feeling is, but I like it. It feels good. Life is good.

A x

'Be completely
humble and gentle;
be patient, bearing
with one another
in love.'

– Ephesians 4:2

My Journal

'There are three things extremely
hard: steel, a diamond and to know
one's self.'
— Benjamin Franklin

'When you realise how
perfect everything is,
you will tilt your head back
and laugh at the sky.'

– Buddha

MONTH 3

Self-Enquiry through Meditation

'DIVINE HAPPINESS,
even the tiniest particle of a grain of it,
never leaves one again; and when one
attains to the essence of things
and finds one's Self
– this is supreme happiness.'

– Anandamayi Ma

Having spent a long time studying the mind through my exploration of hypnosis, I felt I was only tapping into a piece of the puzzle in my quest for inner peace, happiness, acceptance and unconditional love.

When I acknowledged the deep connection between my mind, body and soul, and read more about how our beliefs and our biology are profoundly intertwined, there was a big shift in the direction of my own personal journey. I realised that living my best possible life and truly living in a blissful way was about something far bigger than just my physical health – having chronic pain, I longed for a pain-free life, but that wasn't enough. I also needed a nourishing spiritual life and a healthy emotional life and, most of all, I needed to truly connect with myself, the sacred essence of me that made me who **I am**.

When I learned to meditate, I became more self-aware. I began to get in touch with who I was and what I wanted, but I also became more aware of what was going on in my mind. There is no exact science to how I meditate – it could be called hypnosis, mindfulness, prayer or active relaxation – but the practice of taking this important 'me' time has truly helped me to become still, to make my mind quiet enough that I can pay careful attention to myself.

I learned with practice to notice my own thoughts and to explore the essence of me. During my meditations I would ask my soul for messages. This routine of asking questions and waiting for insights helped me to understand what was going to bring me more personal happiness. It became clear to me during this process that I was constantly searching for signs from outside sources about what paths to take. Somehow, the more I searched outside myself, the more it became clear that all the answers and wisdom were within me.

Sometimes when we are in a dark place it is hard to believe that light is within us. But when we choose not to trust in our instinctive wisdom, we are simply weakening and relinquishing our personal power. So going within during meditation for self-exploration became my biggest source of inspiration and strength, even during dark, painful times.

'The purpose of MEDITATION is to make our mind CALM and PEACEFUL. If our mind is peaceful, we will be free from worries and mental discomfort, and so we will experience TRUE HAPPINESS. But if our mind is not peaceful, we will find it very difficult to be HAPPY, even if we are living in the very best conditions.'

– Kelsang Gyatso

DARE OF THE DAY

Try to be still and connect with the quiet part of your mind, body and soul, the spirit source within that holds all the answers. Sit in silence and become still for a few minutes and, with your journal close by, ask yourself this question:

If you could ask your soul anything, what would you want to know?

....

....

....

....

During my meditation one day, I began a dialogue with my soul. I became aware that I was constantly looking for signs from outside my body. I began to understand I needed to trust my inner being, the voice within me that knows my truth. Suddenly, with this breakthrough of awareness, I could see the infinite spectrum of possibilities for my own life.

Sometimes I felt certain synchronicities and signs were pointers in the right direction, but then I realised I was still looking for external validation for who I needed to be or what I needed to do. I had to trust the voice within.

DARE OF THE WEEK

For the next week, take time each day in meditation to consider the **soul questions** in this section. You might be very surprised by the insights you gain – I know I was.

The biggest realisation for me was that the happiness I was seeking had to come from within. When I let go of the attachment to external sources filling my well of happiness, I became so much more serene.

During meditation, I remember thinking **the end** is actually **the beginning**. If I want to be happy in the end, I need to be happy now – not wait for something or someone to make me happy.

I choose happiness to be my beginning now
and it begins with self.
I am happy now it is a choice.

Try these **soul questions**.

What is going to make me happy?

....

....

....

....

....

Try to meditate or sit in silence and connect with your inner wisdom
and soul.

What do I secretly believe about myself?

....

....

....

....

....

For me this was very powerful. The more I began to see myself from my
own unique perspective, and not through the lens of others, I stopped
trying to change for their benefit. I can now say that I love myself for me
and live on purpose.

What do I want in the end?

....

....

....

....

Let the answer be your beginning – so if you want love, you must feel loved now. Truly embrace what it is to feel loved; focus only on feelings of abundant love not lack of love.

Our souls are full of wisdom. Some believe we have lived many lives and have learned many lessons and this inner knowledge will guide us to find our true path in life. To be more in touch with our souls, we have to reconnect with ourselves. Establishing this connection with yourself is easier than you can imagine. All you have to do is make time for yourself to do absolutely nothing. But do nothing on purpose and do nothing in a mindful way – there is a difference.

By now we have learned to identify the voice of our true self and the voice of the ego, so when receiving a message from your soul, recognise the inner voices and messages that come from your true self and the thoughts that come from your ego.

Some of the thoughts you have at the beginning may have a very negative tone. Be careful of your mind. Become the gatekeeper whom you let into your meditation party. Think of your thoughts like your friends – who you hang around with can either lift you up or leave you drained, so choose carefully what thoughts you fill your mind with. Also remember, just because you have a thought doesn't make it true. It could be part of a script your ego invented – don't believe everything you think!

If you notice your inner voice is critical, negative, judgemental or moving into blame or recrimination, accept this is the ego voice of fear speaking to you. Love is the opposite of fear, so maybe you need to work a little more on self-love and unconditional love. This is OK; accept that you haven't done enough work to tap into your own essence and love yourself without limit.

Love is about letting go of fear and loving this darker side of your personality too. We will explore that further later, but for now let us focus on being in a loving space as you begin this exploration of the true essence of you.

You have your own unique, personality, life experience, perspective and, most importantly, awareness. No one is perfect, but through accepting your imperfections using grace and unconditional love, you can achieve internal peace.

Going within, you will discover how *you* truly see you.

> Remember you are the only you in the world.
> Only you can be you.

Affirming **I am who I am** and you are who you are is liberating, but it doesn't stop there: it is just the beginning. Once you take down those barriers of fear and stop trying to please everyone but yourself, once you begin to start loving from the inside out, you will feel reenergised and plugged in to an inner peace, happiness and bliss that knows no boundaries. This is because you are loved by you. When we are comfortable in our own skin, our beauty radiates.

This practice of self-love truly nourishes the mind, body and soul. Socrates noted that 'the unexamined life is not worth living'. And the practice of asking my **soul questions** has brought me a lot of clarity. This idea isn't new – it takes many forms. The great Indian guru Ramona Maharshi termed it **self-enquiry**. He believed it to be the 'the most sacred of sacred'.

Indeed, it is one of the best ways of helping us along an intentional path of living our life without limit, releasing our fullest personal potential. When we choose to go within we can anchor our true Divine identity and steady our course to move through our day in wholeness and with the confidence to express our uniqueness and creativity – to be who we were born to be. If you follow this process of self-inquiry or asking your **soul questions**, you will allow the light that sparks you from within to ignite.

In Ramana Maharshi's self-enquiry method, the question **Who am I?** has a very special quality because it is an interrogation that makes the mind enter into a state of void. By holding this space within, we are asked to witness what moves in that space. What we observe and notice are the true qualities of our inner being. Honouring this space with the intention of love, compassion, insight and acceptance is very important before asking, in meditation, 'Who am I?'

DARE OF THE MONTH

This month try a new **mindful activity** and explore your inner self. It might take a few attempts before it feels natural so practise over the month ahead.

Self-inquiry does not need to be complicated. The goal of a mindful activity is to bring your thoughts into the present moment. This month, set your intention to practise a little silent reflective time to ask your **soul questions**.

Always start with the intention of love, compassion, insight and acceptance. Ground yourself in these qualities and make time and space to go within.

Begin a meditation practice by sitting for just 20 minutes a day.

Meditation creates change in the brain and behaviour. To begin, first choose your self-inquiry question. A good place to start is **Who am I?**

* Find a comfortable place – sit in a chair, lie down or use a cushion. The important thing is to be comfortable.

* Stay as still as possible. Focus on your belly rising and falling with every breath. You may notice that, almost immediately, you will lose this focus of attention and start following your thinking. That's OK.

* Bring yourself back to the question. To anchor yourself, you can also come back to your breath – again and again, as necessary. When you stay with the breath, even for just one inhalation, celebrate that you are doing really well.

* Simply sense yourself and do not worry about inside or outside or going deeper. Sense that you exist right now, and then stay with that sense of 'I' or 'me'.

* Staying with the self-inquiry question **Who am I?** opens up space. When the answer can come from our intuition, it shows our real nature.

* Stay with the question even when you experience nothing and have no idea who you are. Just ask, who or what part of you doesn't know? Is it your ego that is blocking you answering who you truly are? This question, regardless of what you are experiencing, will bring up some insights.

* Sometimes this process of inquiring can conjure up mental images. Nothing is wrong – just focus on the question again, repeating **Who am I?** with sincerity, as often as possible.

* If you want to try something different, ask the self-enquiry question to different parts of yourself. Ask **Who am I?** to the **soul**, to the **mind**, to the **body** – observe the answer.

* You can practise this over a period of weeks if necessary. Take as long as you need to explore this meditation.

I have my own method when asking **Who am I?** to the mind. I put the 'I,' the thought of the 'I', right in the middle of my head/mind space and just sit with it. (When asking the soul, I imagine being in the heart space, and when I ask the body I feel the question navigating around my body.) Then I ask the question and just surrender. When you do this, you might have the feeling that all your limits dissolve. Or you might find that there is no rational answer – you might want to just surrender to what comes up in the stillness and silence of the self-enquiry. Often a spontaneous inner awareness of who we are will reveal itself or it might take a different, longer path – just allow it to go where it needs to.

This is my method, but the best way to learn about this process is to read Ramana Maharshi's works, many of which contain descriptions of self-enquiry.

'Questioning "Who am I?" within one's mind, when one reaches the heart, the individual "I" sinks crestfallen, and at once reality manifests itself as "I-I". Though it reveals itself thus, it is not the ego "I" but the perfect being, the Self Absolute.'

– Ramana Maharshi

Remember:

❋ This is called practice! To harness the great value in the meditation on 'I-am-ness', start with your daily 20 minutes and think about increasing it in the other 23 hours and 40 minutes of your day. But at the beginning do your 20 minutes and celebrate at the end without any judgement.

❋ It's all about growing in awareness. Awareness is another name for **you**. Since you are awareness, there is no need to attain or cultivate it. All you have to do is give up being aware of other things and just be willing to do the work of asking the question and becoming aware. Pure awareness alone is the self.

❋ You have within you all that is required to gain the key to your infinite self. You have VIP membership to a club with guaranteed endless benefits. It is a place of endless love and boundless peace and happiness. Simply follow the steps and stay true to yourself.

MONTHLY REVIEW

JOURNAL WORK

With the intention of love, compassion, insight and acceptance, ask these **soul questions** in meditation:

Who am I?

_____

_____

_____

_____

What is going to make me happy?

_____

_____

_____

_____

What do I want in the end?

....

....

....

....

What do I secretly believe about myself?

....

....

....

....

MEDITATION

This month we explore self-inquiry and going inside and just being with a centring soul question. I have devised a meditation to help you connect with your inner self. This one is gently guided and then has 10 minutes of relaxing music so you can enter your own sacred space and ask your soul question. A bell will sound at the end of the time and you will be gently guided back from meditation. You will find the link on my website www.andreahayes.ie at Month 3 of the media section under Mind, Body, Soul Journal.

JOURNAL REMINDERS

I always include 10 minutes after each meditation to allow some time for a little journal work or 'free writing' about the experience. You can use the blank pages at the end of this chapter or your private journal to do this. For me this was a win-win, as sometimes on reflection the journal work was just as insightful as the meditation itself. Remember, your journal work is not judgemental, so express yourself in any way you choose, whether it's in words, pictures or whatever way feels right to you.

✳ Just **focus** on the experience of asking the soul question. You can even write the question again or simply allow the concept of 'I-am-ness' to fill the page

✳ By **writing routinely** after the meditation you will become clear about your own growth as you explore the different reactions of the mind, body and soul to the questions. This is all-important information for your journey into knowing your true self.

✳ What I wish I'd known when I began my journey is how effective a **support** my journal has been to me. It might not seem important yet, but your writing will aid your personal search for self-enquiry. Your journal may be the map you require on your journey to knowing what your life purpose is.

✳ **Be patient** but know that with regular practice it only takes six weeks to create a new neural pathway – once you get into the practice of meditation your life will change forever.

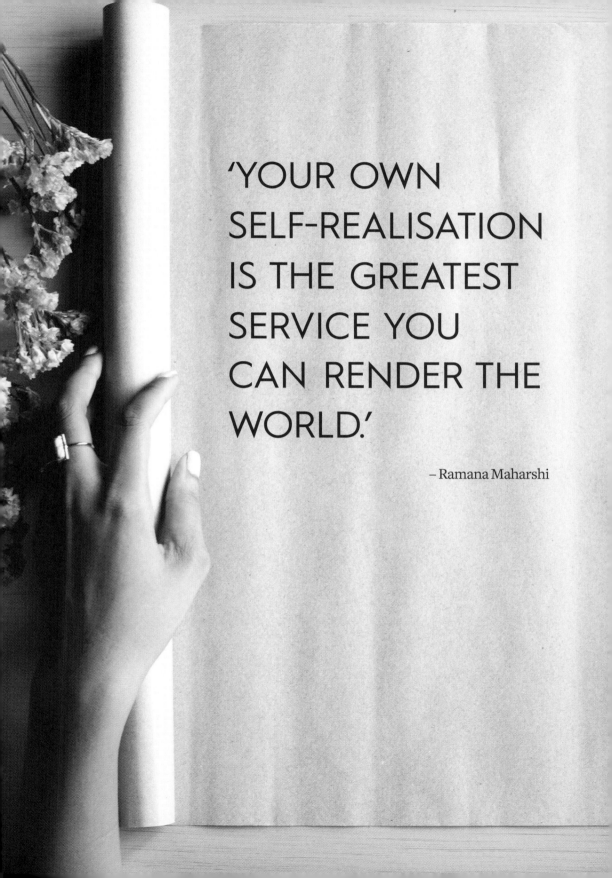

'YOUR OWN SELF-REALISATION IS THE GREATEST SERVICE YOU CAN RENDER THE WORLD.'

– Ramana Maharshi

My Journal Extract

I am feeling so energised by this incredible work I am doing since I gave up the burden of comparisons and began to simply focus on me, myself and I. It feels so wonderfully refreshing. I was walking today with my dog, Dash, mindful walking, staying with a centring thought of 'I am happiness', and I just seemed to be glowing. Without having to worry about all the things that bring me happiness, or all the things or achievements I think I need to be happy, I just embraced happiness fully in my mind, body and soul and simply felt 'happy'. It seems too simplistic writing it now, but that simple act of switching off the internal worry warrior and not thinking of what will bring happiness but just being *happy is simply powerful.*

I keep thinking of the Shakespeare quote, 'to be or not to be'. I know the context in his play is totally different, but today, for me, it seemed to resonate – to be happy or not to be happy: it is our choice. We can all choose what we can be. I can be anything I want. That is such a powerful thought.

The feeling I have at the moment is hard to describe. I feel like I am viewing everything in my world in a new way, or maybe I am just choosing to block out the stuff that wastes my time and brings me into a negative space. The space I am in feels so positive and illuminating, and I am feeling so happy. I feel the things I am spending my time on at the moment are bringing me so much peace, and this feeling of peace is transferred into all my work – it is seeping into all my conversations, my thoughts, my work, my life! This feels good. I want to bottle this feeling and space and hold onto it, as it feels right for me.

The more work I do on myself, the more I understand what makes me happy and the more happiness I seem to attract into my life.

A x

'You can't pour from an empty cup; take care of yourself first.'

–Unknown

My Journal

'*Spiritual progress is like detoxification. Things have to come up in order to be released. Once we have asked to be healed, then our unhealed places are forced to the surface.*'

– Marianne Williamson

'The only **LIMIT** to our **REALIZATION** of tomorrow will be our **DOUBTS** of **TODAY**.'

– Franklin D. Roosevelt

MONTH 4

Awareness of Inner Voices and Big Mind

'What a liberation to realize that the "voice in my head" is not who I am. "Who am I, then?" The one who sees that.'

– Eckhart Tolle

Have you ever experienced a 'transition state'?

This journey is all about positively reframing your thinking and your attitude to yourself. When you think about being the best you, things like diet and exercise are typically the first to come to mind. However, wellness isn't just about the physical body. We are trying to reach equilibrium of your mind, body and soul – they are all interconnected and affect each other tremendously.

As we are learning, it is essential to maintain a healthy balance within this trinity by nurturing your whole self, including your physical, mental, emotional and spiritual needs: the aim is to cultivate a mind-body-soul balance. This new way of living might require some change. We all experience transitions during our lives – you could be in the middle of one right now without even realising.

These life shifts change our awareness and our consciousness. Moving from an old, familiar reality into a new reality is a transitional state – when you are temporarily poised between the old and the new.

They typically occur when, for example:

* we move job or lose our employment,

* we leave a long-term relationship,

* any type of 'traumatic' event occurs where we don't know what the future will bring – a worrying health diagnosis, perhaps,

* a close family member or friend dies,

* we become a parent or our family expands,

* we retire from a job,

* a new relationship or friendship begins or ends,

Doing the work we are exploring in this book may shift your awareness and bring you into a transitional state of change. You might feel 'in between' the old way you once operated and the beginning of your new life, with endless possibilities as you feel more confident moving in the direction of your true calling.

When life shifts for us and we experience transitions, even happy ones, they can often stir up our emotions and memories or bring up mixed feelings. These times of change can be stressful. It's natural to feel comfortable surrounded by what we know, so when the familiar is falling away it can be very disorienting. It's not all bad, though – sometimes shifts are like being on an emotional rollercoaster, exciting and scary at the same time. We are often imagining the bright possibilities of our future yet we know our past so it can feel like our sense of self is in question.

From my own experience, during my transition to this new place of awareness, I had to embrace my inner darkness to achieve the illumination and spiritual balance I needed to become an integrated, whole person, mind, body and soul. I understood that to deny any part of the self would only create disharmony.

It is by embracing *all* of the self that we earn the freedom to choose what we do in this world. The path to self-awareness during this journaling journey will reveal many new aspects of your true self, and you need to embrace all these parts of your personality to fully grow. It can be easy to live on autopilot; however, I am asking you now to make a shift, dig underneath your surface and embrace *all* parts of your being.

As long as we keep hiding behind a disguise, masquerading and projecting a false sense of self to the world, we cannot truly live on purpose and embrace all we can be. It is only when we discover what parts of our mind are pulling the strings in our life that we can step into our greatest self.

Discovering this darker part of our own personality is what Swiss psychiatrist and psychoanalyst Carl Jung called the shadow – he writes about this in *Psychology of the Unconscious*. The shadow contains all the parts of ourselves that we have tried to hide or deny. Most of us set out on the path to personal growth because we want to know ourselves in a deeper way.

According to Jung, we have a persona and a shadow self. The **Persona** is what we would like to be and how we would like to be seen by the world. The word *persona* is derived from a Latin word that literally means 'mask'. On the other hand, the **Shadow** forms part of the unconscious mind and is composed of repressed ideas, instincts, impulses, weaknesses, desires, perversions and embarrassing fears. This is often described as the darker side of the psyche.

I have written about the power of the mind and controlling our inner dialogue and self-talk, but we can go deeper with this. Often we resist looking long and hard at where negative messages manifest out of fear: fear of discovering someone we can't live with.

> We believe we are the messages we tell our
> bodies and our minds.

Sometimes we self-sabotage relationships, diets, our career, dreams and even our life goals because we believe we are the disturbing internal messages we tell our bodies and our minds: 'I'm not good enough. I'm not lovable. I do not deserve. I'm not worthy.'

DARE OF THE DAY

Today, take some quiet time to yourself to tune in to your self-talk and inner dialogue.

What negative internal messages do you tell yourself?

....

....

....

....

Often it's during self-reflection that these repressed fears and messages surface. These voices can be so deep that the only way we can deal with them is to either hide or deny them, occasionally giving them some self-talk time. We become imposters in our own lives, wearing masks, playing a part, living according to this false script to hide our authentic selves.

It is important to give all these voices an outlet; we can't change what we do not accept. This shadow part of our subconscious holds the essence of who we are – the good and the bad, the dark and the light.

Why is it that certain parts of our core are the parts that often take centre stage? Why have these personality traits or voices become dominant and run our lives? Sometimes these parts of our persona may have developed in our childhood to protect us and help us survive, for example, a voice of 'fear' that stems from being left alone in hospital as a child. But we may not need that part of our personality anymore.

DARE OF THE WEEK

This week, try to take time every day to truly examine your own personality. This is similar to tuning in to your self-talk, but you want to go a bit deeper. Think about it: you probably have never questioned why you act the way you do. Now is the time to start. Below are some searching **soul questions**. Take one each day, think about it as you go through your day and journal on any insights the exploration might reveal.

What is the true essence of my personality?

....

....

....

Have I ever questioned why I act the way I do?

....

....

....

What negative messages is my shadow communicating?

....

....

....

Can I hear the *voice of oneness?*

....

....

....

Did I do anything today that didn't feel authentic or true for me?

....

....

....

What am I most afraid of? Is the voice of 'fear' stifling my life?

....

....

....

What is my inner voice saying to me today? Is it positive or negative?

....

....

....

While I was studying to become a spiritual companion, I was introduced to a process that I found very insightful and was one of the most effective ways to reflect on my own shadow side. It is called 'Big Mind: Change Your Perspective, Change Your Life', founded by Dennis Genpo Merzel Roshi. It allows you to go inside your mind and give your different personas and personalities voices, which gives you an opportunity to explore what is directing your internal self-talk and where those voices are coming from. It appears very simple but is considered a profound process by many and a pathway to find your true self. It can be explored more on www.bigmind.org. Ken Wilber, the author and philosopher often referred to as the 'Einstein of consciousness', describes it as 'an astonishingly original, profound, and effective path for waking up, or seeing one's true nature'.

Here is my interpretation of the process and the way I use it. Follow the steps outlined and try it for yourself.

BIG MIND

According to Dennis Genpo Merzel Roshi, the self can take on many personalities. These live in our unconsciousness and often emerge as the internal voices we hear in self-talk. Although sometimes they may be long buried, he feels it is important to give all of these innumerable voices, or aspects, within us an outlet. Once we acknowledge them, we can then learn how they affect us and we can be more in control of our true selves.

To get a clearer picture of how my shadow voices operate, I decided to imagine I was preparing for a radio show and I had to interview all of these voices as guests – imagine it as a panel discussion.

I needed to see how many guests I might have and, to be honest, I wasn't sure until I started to do the research, as I would ahead of any show. Then I needed to get to know the voices and see what their points of view might be so I would know what questions to ask them on air. For any radio show it is important that all guests get equal air time, so I also needed to make sure no one was dominating it.

Name of show – Revealing Who Andrea Hayes Truly Is

Guests – Voices of the Self:

1. The voice of the Protector and Controller

2. The voice of Fear

3. The voice of the Sceptic

4. The voice of the Victim

5. The voice of the Damaged Self

6. The voice of the Fixer

7. The voice of the Vulnerable and Innocent Child

8. The voice of Desire

9. The voice of the Seeking Mind

10. The voice of the Divine Self, Big Mind

I imagined the process just as I would for my own radio show, *Sunshine Meets* on Sunshine 106.8. The first question I ask is, 'When were you born and can you tell us a little about yourself?' This gives me an opportunity to discover where the guest is coming from. Then I explore big moments in the guest's life and how things are for them now. For this exercise, I wanted to do the same with each voice – this is extremely personal but it is worth exploring.

Here's an example from my own journal:

PROTECTOR AND CONTROLLER

Born: *In childhood when I was in hospital*

Important moments: *Felt I was left alone and needed to rely on myself.*

FEAR

Born: *In childhood fear of being abandoned*

Important moments: *Felt I was left alone when my older siblings emigrated at a young age.*

During this process I interviewed each voice to see what it had to say. It might seem a little weird, but this process of inner dialoguing with the voices and seeing what comes up for you has its roots in Voice Dialogue, a technique that has been used in Western psychology for years as a means of dealing with aspects of ourselves we have disowned.

You might find, as I did, that some aspects of ourselves have never been awakened, like Desire or Seeking Mind, and other voices, like Fear or Sceptic, seem to be always trying to take up all the airtime because they feel their story is more important than anyone else's!

Then, as the presenter of your show, you need to reframe the voices and challenge them. Instead of being stuck in the important moment from the past when fear was born, I needed to transition it into a useful place in my future. So I looked to give the voice a new job, see its usefulness. Fear now is no longer something undesirable for me; I see it having a useful function that warns the Self of imminent danger. Instead of allowing it to take over my life I am able to say, 'Thank you for the past, for all the work you did when I was a child, but I am older now and I don't need to see everything as fearful or hold onto that fear of abandonment.'

By going through each voice and exploring its story, you will be amazed by the insights that emerge – you just need to listen to them and give them a chance to get some airtime. The idea is to recognise the voices and, as the presenter of the show, ensure that you now have a deeper understanding of where they come from. Then, just like a radio show, you can choose to listen further to the voices, cut the interview short, turn down the volume if needed, play some music for distraction, go to a break or indeed change the channel altogether. As the presenter, you are in control, and in this role, you are your true and unique self, the mind, body and soul.

When you learn how to navigate your inner voices and harness them to create the life you want, you can really start to transition to a new state of awareness, and this opens the door to the freedom to live the life you want. When you acknowledge and confirm that you are the voice of the true and unique self – the mind, body and soul or the Divine or Big Mind self – you no longer identify with the other ego voices of the self. It is important to remember that our internal thoughts are only thoughts: they do not define who we are.

'It is better to **conquer yourself** than to **win** a thousand battles. Then the **victory** is yours. It cannot be taken from you.'

– Buddha

DARE OF THE MONTH

Be the presenter of your own Big Mind radio show. Here are some suggestions for your guests. Choose the ones that resonate with you or come up with your own.

Competition Follower
Divine Self
Fear Innocent
Sceptic *Fixer*
Desire
ENVY MIND Victim
Vulnerability Damaged self
Seeking CHILD
Jealousy Freedom
Compassion Guardian
Master

Name of show:

Guests:

1. The voice of ....

2. The voice of ....

3. The voice of ....

4. The voice of ....

5. The voice of ....

6. The voice of ....

7. The voice of ....

8. The voice of ....

Now, begin to talk to each voice, exploring their story.

1. The voice of ....

Born: ....

Important moments: ....

2. The voice of ....

Born: ....

Important moments: ....

3. The voice of ....

Born: ....

Important moments: ....

4. The voice of ....

Born: ....

Important moments: ....

5. The voice of ....

Born: ....

Important moments: ....

6. The voice of ....

Born: ....

Important moments: ....

7. The voice of ....

Born: ....

Important moments: ....

8. The voice of ....

Born: ....

Important moments: ....

'Better keep yourself clean
and bright; you are the
window through which you
must see the world.'

– George Bernard Shaw

MONTHLY REVIEW

JOURNAL WORK

Once you have had a dialogue with your shadow voices for the first time, you can use a simpler practice. If you already have a regular meditation routine, begin by assuming your usual posture. If you're new to meditation, find a comfortable upright position (sitting in a chair is sufficient), take a few deep breaths and relax. Then simply choose one voice to dialogue with for a set period of time, like 10 minutes, then allow the voice to fill the silence, listen and accept what comes up.

You can journal your experience with each voice, like you are taking notes on what they had to say on the pages at the end of this chapter or in your personal writing space. While doing this, you can talk aloud to your guest voice if you are in a safe and private place where you won't be disturbed.

MEDITATION

I have devised a meditation to help you explore your inner voices – if you want to try my guided exercise for Big Mind then go to Month 4 on my website at www.andreahayes.ie/media.

My Journal Extract

I am still a little uneasy about what came up for me in my Shadow Audit. I wasn't surprised by a few voices – I am aware that I can use the strong, angry side of myself for protection so, although I wasn't comfortable with that voice, it didn't surprise me. But the one that I can't stop thinking about is the voice of passion. I saw passion as a negative thing – I couldn't give it much of a voice as I would be worried about where it might lead me, so I tended to close down that voice to protect myself. It is very strange. On reflection, I wondered if I am truly being me if I am not allowing time to explore and give a voice to my passions.

My immediate reaction was that I didn't want to think about it too much, but then that is just pushing it back into the shadows. It was so interesting to see those insights into my personality. I am exhausted after the day and I am wondering if I did the process tomorrow would I get different results? So I plan to do the Big Mind process again and explore the voices for the next little while and journal on the insights and revelations. I felt doing it in the group today was a little limiting, as I felt a bit judged – or is that just me projecting my own inner judgements about myself externally onto others? It shouldn't matter what others think at all – I need to only focus on within.

I have to say, while I am not sure about Big Mind, it is a useful and more detailed exploration of self-talk and the inner critic. What is interesting is the amount of childhood voices that emerged. In a way, it felt like a spring clean. I am happy I started clearing out the crap, but it's going to take me longer than expected, and I am exhausted but, at the same time, I feel lighter and brighter and happy with the progress.

Maybe I will do a voice a day. I am not sure but I know there is more work to do.

Good night,

A x

'If we're **growing,** we're always going to be out of our **comfort zone'**

– John Maxwell

My Journal

_____

_____

_____

_____

_____

_____

_____

_____

_____

_____

_____

_____

_____

'The best and most beautiful things in the world cannot be seen or even touched. They must be felt with the heart.'

– Helen Keller

_____

_____

_____

'I don't want to be at the
mercy of my emotions.
I want to use them,
to enjoy them and
to dominate them.'

– Oscar Wilde

MONTH 5

Take Control of Your Wheel of Emotions

'Let's not forget
that the LITTLE
EMOTIONS are
the great captains
of our lives and
we OBEY THEM
without realizing it.'

– Vincent van Gogh

Our journey through life should be all about expansion and growth. As human and spiritual beings we evolve as we go through different phases of our own self-awareness. In order to become aware of the self, we need to develop a deep understanding of our emotions. We need to focus not on what we are looking at but on what lens we are seeing things through.

The lens through which we view our experiences depends on our emotional response and our perception of the world around us. If we can adjust our focus and understand our emotional triggers, it can influence how we experience our world and also shed light on how we can know the self more completely.

The intention to be aligned to what one is feeling is empowering. Instead of trying to suppress, ignore or even reject the emotions we are feeling, we need to embrace them and learn through our responses. It is important to adopt and understand a new vocabulary that will help to express and share how we are feeling in a constructive way, as well as analyse the role our emotions they play in our life.

Emotions come from the Latin term *emovere* meaning 'moving'.

In general, the emotions that precede thought are a direct, visceral response to how our life is flowing – we are moved by our immediate situation – and these are considered primary emotions. **Primary emotions** are those that we feel as a first response to a situation. Typical primary emotions are **love, joy, surprise, fear, sadness, anger, disgust, shame, pride.** An example is the feeling of happiness you have upon seeing a loved one.

Secondary emotions always appear after primary emotions. They are much more complex and may be caused directly by a primary emotion – for example, where the fear of a threat turns to anger that fuels the body for fight or flight; or you feel anger and then perhaps feel ashamed of that anger afterwards. Master Yoda in *Star Wars* explained it perfectly: 'Fear leads to anger, anger leads to hate, hate leads to suffering.'

DARE OF THE DAY

Can you identify if an emotion is primary or secondary? Just for today, try to monitor the types of emotional responses you have to the situations that occur. Even try it for an hour!

First, ask yourself if this feeling is a direct response to an event. If it is then it's a **primary emotion** – these can be intense and fade quickly.

Secondary emotions are more unconscious and habitual – they tend to linger long after the event has happened. These will tell us a lot about how we processed the original event on an unconscious level.

For example, take a situation where you are late for work. Your primary emotions are frustration and anger. Your secondary emotions are disgust and anxiety. Your emotional response is to not feel good enough.

Situation:

....

Emotional Response:

....

Was it a primary emotion? What was the emotion?

....

Was it a secondary emotion? What was the emotion?

....

Explore the emotional response:

....

....

....

I began to see my emotional response to situations in a whole new way, and by journaling through the experience, I received new wisdom, clarity and self-awareness. These became the cornerstones to improving my emotional intelligence, and indeed my wellbeing.

For me, this was a very liberating experience: learning to navigate my emotions helped me become more relaxed when dealing with life's highs and lows. I developed strength and grace from understanding that my emotional response was just that: it was mine to own. Every day we face challenges, disappointments and triumphs, but the key is how we decide to react. I began each day thinking **'I have an opportunity today to practise being stronger and more robust in my reactions to my own wellspring of feelings and emotions.'**

Our emotions are to be valued and respected. Many people try to pick the emotions that are pleasant and ignore or deny the ones that are unpleasant. I have learned we must express our emotions in order to heal them. All emotions can be transformed by love; we just need to make a conscious intention to do so. This forms the basic understanding of evolutionary psychology: our job is to accept all of our emotions, both pleasant and unpleasant, and understand them as important messengers delivering important insights into our minds and how our lives have unfolded. Even negative emotions can be a catalyst for a positive transformational shift.

For example, I discovered when I did my version of the Big Mind process that I use anger as a protection. Initially, I would have said I really didn't enjoy feeling angry, but I learned that anger is quite a healthy response to being emotionally or physically violated. It helps to give you the energy and direction to activate and protect yourself or the people you care about. When you are angry you are ready to act (the fight or flight response mentioned above) and this is a completely natural and healthy response in the body. Despite what I once believed about anger, it has been a healthy emotion for me to have in the past and it has also been negative.

It is important for us to be able to categorise the shades of basic emotions and know their positive and negative effects in our own personalities and lives.

The term **emotional intelligence** has been discussed and written about since the 1960s. In simple terms, it means your ability to be aware of, control and express your emotions. Being emotionally intelligent allows you to better understand not only yourself but others too.

Just as with our own inner chatter and self-talk, we need to make a conscious intention to face our emotions in an honest, compassionate,

'EMOTIONAL INTELLIGENCE, more than any other factor, more than I.Q. or expertise, accounts for

85% to 90%

of success at work ... I.Q. is a threshold competence. You need it, but it doesn't make you a star. Emotional intelligence can.'

– Warren G. Bennis

non-judgemental way. We need to accept all emotions and all feelings, both negative and positive. Without the ability to understand and control our emotions, we are unable to thrive and grow. It's like building on an unstable foundation: it will be impossible to achieve true balance in our mind, body and soul if we cannot acknowledge our true feelings and emotions – it's the true path to self-transformation.

Therefore, when going on this journey of self-awareness, it is so important to utilise and perfect the emotional tools we need to manage our **thoughts**, **feelings** and **behaviours**.

By paying attention to all three areas we can begin to learn and deeply understand what weakens our selves and what makes us stronger. After a while, it becomes second nature to be in touch with your feelings and you might notice that you emerge from your daily struggles even wiser and more resilient than before.

The **goal** is to learn to challenge your thoughts and be more mindful of them. Often you experience certain emotions because you've had them before in the same types of situations: it's become a habit. Over time, the practice of recognising and challenging your emotions can help you reduce their effects and this can create positive change in our behaviours. This awareness can help you stay in touch with your truth in a situation long enough to act on the reality of what is happening in a healthy way.

A simple way to start the process of recognising your feelings and emotions and determining their sources is by using a mood chart.

DARE OF THE WEEK

Try the **mood chart** on the next page for a week, or even on and off this month, and see how insightful it can be. By monitoring your feelings and emotions you will start to recognise the links between the people you are around, the environment you are in, the thoughts you are having and the feelings that occur from different daily scenarios.

DAILY MOOD CHART

TIME	LOVE	JOY	SURPRISE	FEAR	SADNESS	ANGER
6 a.m. – 8 a.m.						
8 a.m. – 10 a.m.						
10 a.m. – 12 p.m.						
12 p.m. – 2 p.m.						
2 p.m. – 4 p.m.						
4 p.m. – 6 p.m.						
6 p.m. – 8 p.m.						
8 p.m. – 10 p.m.						
10 p.m. – 12 a.m.						
12 p.m. – 2 a.m.						

DISGUST   PRIDE   SHAME   OTHER   NOTES

HOW TO FILL IN YOUR MOOD CHART:

  ❋ Every two hours record the emotions you have experienced.

  ❋ Make a note about what was happening during that time.

  ❋ You can rate the intensity of the feeling on a scale of 1–10 if you want extra insight.

I found this to be really helpful. It can be very revealing to notice how environments, situations, people and interactions in our day-to-day lives can affect how we feel. For example, I woke up at 7 a.m. feeling love for my family, joy for my fresh coffee and overall in good spirits. Then I noticed I felt frustrated, anxious and not good enough. I realised this was a reaction to 10 minutes of social media.

Mood tracking can be a powerful technique when we are having difficulty identifying the source of our negative emotions. The cause of our mood change might be difficult to detect during our busy lives, but patterns will emerge and we can start to see what pushes our buttons and what situations we react to in negative or positive ways. Remember to always review the chart at the end of the day and consider journaling about your insights.

To help you explore your relationship with your moods, take some inspiration from psychologist Robert Plutchik's **wheel of emotions**. On the chart opposite, you can see he uses colours and combinations of emotions. This diagram beautifully depicts the relationships between each emotion in the form of a spectrum. This can be useful to express how you are feeling – even if the exact word to describe your emotion isn't on the spectrum, look at what emotion is closest to it. Having this wheel as a reference can be very useful when you are journaling about your mood chart.

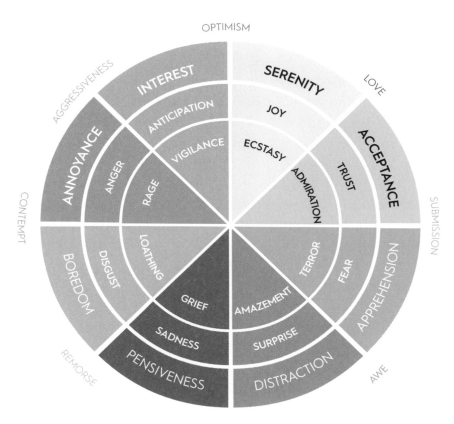

To help you fill in your mood chart, follow my simple **ABC** formula.

A

Accept and **acknowledge** your feelings and emotions. In addition to identifying how you are truly feeling, you can also note that this is an area for change if you do not like the emotional response.

B

Be aware and **build** your insights. Building mental insight and strength is similar to building physical strength. You are exercising a mental muscle every time you become aware of your emotions and feelings – you won't realise how strong you are until you need it the most.

C

Control, consider and remain **calm.** Controlling your mind can be your best asset or your biggest enemy. Sometimes our minds can overthink things or, worse still, try to control every outcome when often you need to let go and let things happen. Consider your past experiences when thinking about your emotional reactions: you might be feeling the way you do because of something that happened to you in the past. Finally, remain calm under emotional pressure. Challenge yourself to take a deep breath and count to ten. You'll feel calmer, stronger and ready to face any situation.

Remember, **don't suppress or deny** any emotions, just acknowledge them and stop blaming others or circumstances.

We need to understand that **an emotion is not bad.** An insight into our own behaviour is always present in everything we feel and this is a gift when we can manage and understand our emotions.

* Tracking your moods can help you to work out what **positively** and **negatively** affects your mental wellbeing. You can then take steps to avoid, change or prepare for negative situations.

* If you notice particular **people** or **places** cause you to feel certain negative emotions, you need to become aware of these toxic triggers

and, instead of taking their negativity to heart, learn to set boundaries around this trigger and not to engage and be affected by it.

* See how sensitive you are to things that often don't matter. By tracking your moods you can learn to **let go** of the little things. If you notice that you are very sensitive to small annoyances or what other people do or say, you might want to consciously ignore them and not allow it to affect your day. Otherwise you will end up devoting too much time and energy to things that, ultimately, don't matter. Practise adjusting your attitude so that you don't stress about the small stuff; learn to take everyday stresses in your stride.

* Once you have pinpointed **when** you felt the emotion during your day, you can work out **what** exactly you felt, and then you can begin to understand **why** you felt that way and if **where** or **who** you were with at the time had an impact on your emotions. That will give you a good picture and through journaling you can delve deeper into the feeling, and maybe even into your subconscious, and make sense of what is really at play.

DARE OF THE MONTH

Learning to identify and understand your emotions is another important part of becoming emotionally and mentally aware of who you truly are. You may not be able to control what life throws at you, but you always have a choice about how you react. This is something we all need to work at, and the more we practise, the easier it gets. If you can try to observe your emotions for 21 days then it becomes a habit. Monitor your daily moods and see if you can spot a pattern. You can copy the chart from page 128-129 into your own personal writing space or create your own way of recording your moods, like keeping a note on your phone. Review after 21 days and reflect on what you have learned.

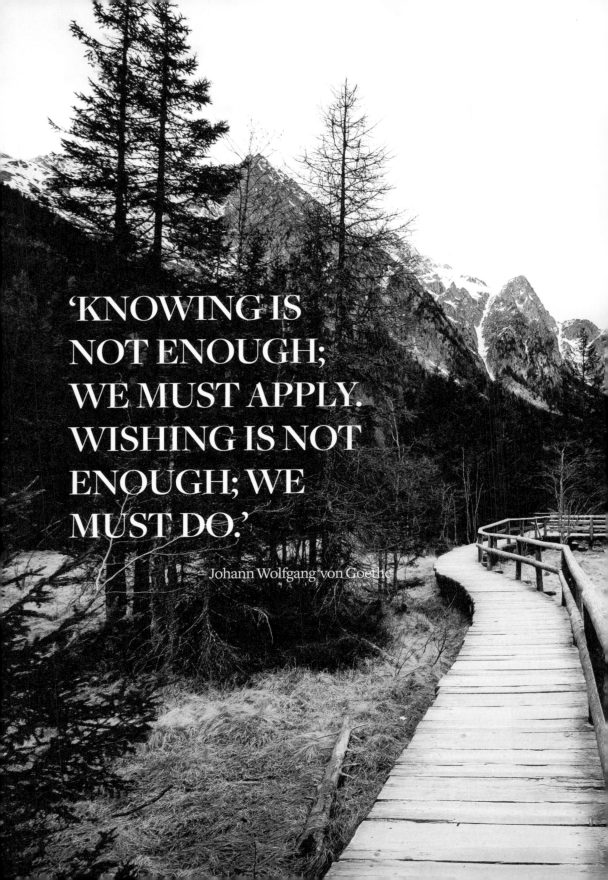

'KNOWING IS NOT ENOUGH; WE MUST APPLY. WISHING IS NOT ENOUGH; WE MUST DO.'

– Johann Wolfgang von Goethe

MONTHLY REVIEW

JOURNAL WORK

Track your thoughts and feelings in your journal. Writing can help you to understand what may have caused you to experience these emotions and it is also a great way to relieve stress associated with your feelings. Ask yourself these **soul questions**.

My biggest emotional challenge is:

....

....

....

I notice the feeling of happiness grows when I:

....

....

....

I need to stop stressing about:

....

....

....

When I am feeling low, the nicest thing I could do or say to myself is:

....

....

....

....

I feel peaceful in my mind, body and soul when I am:

....

....

....

What have I learned from mood mapping?

....

....

....

Have I identified anyone who pulls my strings emotionally?

....

....

....

MEDITATION

This month I have devised a hypnosis relaxation that is for emotional healing and unlocking emotions. Listen to it and see how you can become aware of your own emotional triggers. It is a gentle hypnosis that will also help you to relax and release any emotional baggage from your day. You will find it at Month 5 of my Mind, Body, Soul Journal *at www.andreahayes.ie.*

My Journal Extract

Mood monitoring has been really interesting today. I remember starting my day in a very upbeat and positive way. I went to mass, which I really enjoyed as I hadn't been able to go for a while with work and other commitments, and I was driving to a meeting afterwards feeling really energised – I was actually singing in the car and buzzing with this positive feeling. I pulled in to the garage to get some diesel and my phone rang, so I parked and took the call.

I had a conversation with a family member about a situation that has been going on for a few weeks, and when I finished and got back into the car for my journey ahead, it took about 15 minutes to notice how 'in my head' I was and that my mood had totally changed. I was feeling deflated, drained, anxious and a little angry. It was so useful naming and recognising the feelings and exploring why I felt the way I did.

I could see the anger at the other person on the phone was projection. The very thing I was angry with the person for was a fault deep within myself. I felt that person was trying to control the situation, which I didn't like, but I can see now it is really me that has control issues and my anger is a reflection of a silenced part of my personality, so being aware of that projection helped me send that person love and totally change the energy around my feelings.

Then I had to admit the whole family situation was draining me and, ultimately, I didn't like it or want to really deal with it, so I have decided to move away from it and not let it affect me as much as it clearly has been. I am going to journal about my feelings and keep an eye on how I am handling it over the next few weeks.

Once I could see why my mood changed, I could detach from the new feelings and reclaim my joy – it felt good.

A x

My Journal

_____

_____

_____

_____

_____

_____

_____

_____

_____

_____

_____

_____

'You can't go back and change the beginning, but you can start where you are and change the ending.'
– C. S. Lewis

_____

_____

'EVERY CHILD IS AN ARTIST. THE PROBLEM IS HOW TO REMAIN AN ARTIST ONCE WE GROW UP.'

– Pablo Picasso

MONTH 6

Connect with Your Creativity

'IMAGINATION is more important than knowledge ... For while knowledge defines all we currently know and understand, imagination points to all we might yet DISCOVER AND CREATE.'

– Albert Einstein

As we journey through this process together, I hope that you are you beginning to 'wake up' and acknowledge the state of constant semi-sleep that might have had you stuck in a rut of your daily grind – maybe you felt caught in a cycle, doing the same established routine over and over again, which served to perpetuate the same feelings of being unfulfilled, exhausted and often completely unmotivated to make changes.

Well, there is good news, something I think can help you get your mojo back! Just like sleep is essential to feel rested and excited about the day ahead, I believe creative expression is an essential way to unwind and de-stress, but also, more importantly, I feel it could hold the key to your heart's desire and your true calling in life.

> Myth: creativity is elusive, something that only a few of us can tap into.

Creativity forms the bedrock of our imagination and it is a gift inside every one of us. We just need to open the portal and allow our imagination to connect to our inner secret world of wonder and awe.

Creativity for me is a spiritual activity; it has really helped me to connect to my soul work and life passion. Look upon your imagination as a genie inside your mind, willing to grant your wishes. It is the seat of your inner child, the artist, the Divine creator and your innate dreamer – in many ways it will be your greatest resource and ally as you venture on your journey to find what truly ignites your passion.

Simply becoming aware of our own creativity enables us to begin exploring solutions to our own transformation. Part of this change is rediscovering the concept of the **inner child**. All children are naturally creative. Think back to your own childhood, or focus on the early years of your own child's life, when their imagination was wild and free and they believed in magic and miracles. We need to harness this energy to forge ahead with our own metamorphosis.

Creativity is the power of the imagination to transform. We are all blessed with this amazing capacity for self-renewal. Start now with the intention that nothing is impossible. The real key to turning **imagination into reality** is acting as if the imagined scene were real and already accomplished.

Sometimes, to have that breakthrough moment, you need to think about nothing, doodle, daydream or just allow your mind to drift.

Neuroscientists suggest that the secret to breakthroughs lies in our ability to switch between two modes, the focused and the meandering. It is said that Albert Einstein had a sudden epiphany of discovery regarding his special theory of relativity in one such breakthrough moment.

The **creativity** that we're looking for is already there. We all have the ability to think creatively and to express ourselves creatively. Don't be fooled, though: we need to nurture and enhance our creativity in order for it to grow and bloom.

And being creative is good for your mental health! A prominent creativity researcher and proponent of creativity for all, Ruth Richards of Saybrook University and Harvard Medical School, coined the term **everyday creativity**. Researchers who focus on everyday creativity, or ways to nurture and bring out the creativity in people, have proven it has many wellbeing benefits and that there is a crucial link between creativity and mental health.

In other words, making time for creative activities is literally therapy for your mind. We can all benefit from making it our intention to tap into our creativity and use our imagination. It might surprise you to read that you have already started to flex your creative muscles by journaling. Creative writing has been proven to improve problem-solving abilities and facilitate creative thinking in different situations. This kind of lateral thinking is incredibly valuable in both personal and professional spheres.

So whether it's gardening, writing, drawing, painting, wood carving, sewing, dancing, singing, poetry or baking, **it is the action of using your creativity that is important, rather than the outlet itself**. However you choose to express your creativity is your choice – remember, it doesn't have to be perfect to have purpose. You just need to choose a way to express it.

Stop the negative mantra:
'I don't have a creative bone in my body.'

Start a positive mantra: 'Every day, I create a space to do truly meaningful, creative work.'

Give yourself permission to be creative without judgement. Think about it: we are all creative every day, taking photos on our phones, creating new recipes – even choosing what to wear in the morning takes your own personal creative touch. Don't allow fear to sap your creative juices; replace judgement and perfectionism with fun and inventiveness, and allow yourself to enter the gateway to your own creative genius.

Metamorphosis: a profound change in form from one stages to the next in the life history of an organism, as from the caterpillar to the pupa and the pupa to the adult butterfly.

When you look up caterpillar in the dictionary or encyclopaedia, it is often described in terms of the butterfly, what it *will be*. So decide today: what will you be? It is time for your metamorphosis. Finding and embodying your true creativity allows you to tap into the realm of your infinite possibility and potential.

DARE OF THE DAY

Many of us have become disconnected from our roots and from the things that truly nourish us on a physical, mental, emotional and spiritual level: namely our creativity. Exploring the inner world of your imagination can be fun, and you can begin to see where you might have lost your everyday creativity.

The **tree of life** exercise is a great way to nurture your imagination. It is very simple – you could even do it with your children while you are borrowing their pens and paper. But don't be fooled by its simplicity – it's a great way to connect with important elements of your past, present and future. You might be surprised by the insights you glean from spending some time on it.

The tree has been used many times as a visual metaphor for life and the growth and development we undergo as we weather the storms of what life can throw at us. This activity allows you to reflect on your life in a fun, creative way, while at the same time labelling aspects of your life that have shaped you into the person you are today. It is a great way to reconnect and remember the people and things that helped you to grow strong and move forward.

You'll find many examples of this exercise online. Here, I'm showing you how I use it, and I have added extra themes and ideas.

Your **tree of life** will be unique to you – what you create will be in harmony with your current self-image and your beliefs about who your authentic self is and what your purpose on this earth is. Only you can decide how your tree will look and what colour and shape it will be. Feel free to change my instructions by adding to it or using fewer of the themes below – get creative and put your own personal spin on it. After all, that's part of the process, so enjoy!

TREE OF LIFE

Make some time to get creative and draw your tree. Use a large piece of paper or cardboard with enough space to fill in what you need to include. When I did this first, I traced around my arm and hand for the structure of the tree, so thinking you can't draw a tree is no excuse! You can create any outline for the tree – just be sure to leave space for all the things listed below. If you like, you can use the template in this book on page 149. As you draw your tree, your attention will be brought to various aspects of your life – you might see things you didn't notice before or see something about yourself more clearly.

Your tree should include the following:

* **Roots:** They represent your past, where you come from. Who do you come from? What are the important things in your history?
  Draw one root for each parent, grandparent, sibling, teacher or person who had great importance in your life. Roots nourish a tree – they are the connections that keep them anchored. These are the people who supported you while growing up and maybe helped form your values. It

doesn't matter what you feel about these people, or if they are not around, just draw a root for each one.

* **Ground:** This represents where you are now in your life. What are the important places in your life now? Who are the important people and what important things are happening now (for example partner, spouse, friend, mentor, job, project, children)?

* **Trunk:** this is the core of **you** – your values, skills and knowledge, the things you can do, the qualities you possess. What makes you the person you are (for example kind, honest, tolerant, hardworking, empathetic, intuitive, funny, reliable, and so on)? What roles do you play in your life (for example mother, sibling, son/daughter, partner, artist, teacher, writer)?

* **Main branches:** these signify the future – your goals, dreams, plans, maybe even the life purpose or special mission you feel drawn to do (for example to have a happy family, to travel, to feel calm, to not worry about money, to become a vet, to have new friends, to get healthy, to write a book, to become a motivational speaker). I recommend including at least five.

* **Offshoot branches:** these represent any important people in your life, from the past and present, who support your hopes and dreams that are on the branches (for example your partner, specific family members or certain friends, a boss, teacher, counsellor or other people of significant influence).

* **Flowers:** these represent each thing in your life that makes you feel good about yourself. Draw a little picture or write a word inside the flower of each thing that makes you feel positive (for example your pet, a hobby, compliments, getting your hair done, eating healthily, more me time).

* **Leaves:** use the image of a leaf to represent significant events in your life. A significant event is anything that changed you or your life in some way. Draw a little picture or write a word inside the leaf of each important event (for example death, marriage, health issue, moving home, emigration, operation, and so on).

* **Fruit:** imagine each piece of fruit representing the gifts you have received from the important, valued people in your life (for example safety, love, support, kindness, education, income, laughter).

* **Fallen fruit:** these can be on the ground or falling from the tree, and these are the gifts you have given and continue to give to others (for example your time, money, advice, prayers, support, love, laughter).

* **Storm clouds:** draw clouds to represent any past hurts and challenges or anything you still hold pain because of – you might even be struggling with something right now (for example conflict with family, illness, loss, grief, lack of support, break-up).

* **Rain:** this represents anything you have learned from the storms, so in the rain leave room to write a few words to represent qualities you used to experience growth despite the storm. With every storm cloud comes rain that nourishes our tree. Can you see any positives from your conflicts (for example strength, determination, self-reliance, self-belief, lessons learned)?

* **Sunshine:** draw a big sun with rays coming out. The sun represents what makes you grow and stand tall, the things you do that have filled you with a new wellspring of passion and excitement. These can be from your past or present or maybe something you have always dreamt of doing (for example education, volunteering, helping others, becoming a parent, learning a new hobby, travelling).

* **The compost pile:** think of how decomposed organic matter can become rich fertiliser! Now, in a space beside your tree, reflect on some of the things in your life that you want to recycle. Compost isn't always pleasant – it can be stinky and decaying – so this list is made up of experiences from the past: trauma, illness, abuse, people or places that no longer relate to you and no longer define you but have been part of your growth and perhaps have caused pain. The compost is stuff we eventually break down, things we learn to reframe and deal with over time. These experiences can act like fertiliser and be a rich part of allowing us to grow into who we are today.

    I placed my list between the ground and the roots, as I had room there, or you could leave it to the side of your tree in a pile, or maybe leave it out altogether. If you want, you can write the experiences and then colour them in with dark pen so they are not legible, as they may include very private memories. This can stir up emotions and you might want to share your experiences with a trained counsellor or close friend if you feel overwhelmed.

SUNSHINE

STORM CLOUDS

RAIN

OFFSHOOT BRANCHES

FLOWERS

LEAVES

FRUIT

MAIN BRANCHES

TRUNK

COMPOST PILE

FALLEN FRUIT

GROUND

ROOTS

Now, I want you to try to journal about just one word. If you want, you can choose a word to describe your **tree of life**. I chose wisdom. Don't think about it too much – be spontaneous, whatever comes to mind – and then in your journal reflect on what that word means to you. How does the word relate to you and your life? Explore the connection. Is this the word you want to go forward with or would you like to choose another centring word?

The word for my tree of life is:

Because:

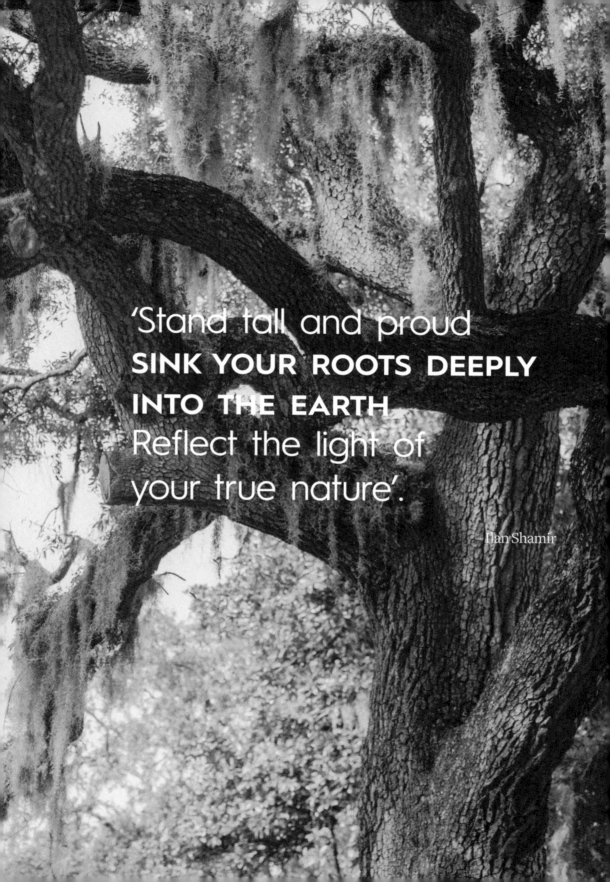

'Stand tall and proud
**SINK YOUR ROOTS DEEPLY
INTO THE EARTH**
Reflect the light of
your true nature'.

– Ilan Shamir

DARE OF THE WEEK

For the next week, choose one of the **soul questions** below each day and journal how you feel about the answer. If you like, you can use your separate writing space and just use below for a sentence prompt. Review them after seven days and see what the entries reveal to you. If you don't have time to write, just look at a question every day and consider it as you go through your daily routine.

What is your passion?

What do you feel you were you born to do?

What creative activity lights you up with joy?

What creative activity would you like to do in the future?

Why?

What do you believe is the meaning of your life?

Are you doing it?

Do you believe your destiny is predetermined or in your hands to shape however you wish?

If you could have any one wish granted what would it be and why?

'While we have the gift of life,
it seems to me the only tragedy
is to allow part of us to die
– *whether it is our spirit, our
creativity or our glorious
uniqueness.*'

– Gilda Radner

DARE OF THE MONTH

Explore your everyday creativity; try for a month to see the extraordinary in the ordinary each day. Make it your intention to bring passion, energy and creativity into your day – for example, cook creatively by adapting a recipe, declutter your house in a creative way and make new space, start a new creative course, plant a vegetable or herb box in your garden, start drawing or painting to flex your creative muscles. The possibilities to be more creative are limitless – the important thing is to be creative on purpose this month and see what new talents reveal themselves to you.

I choose to be creative this month by:

....

....

MONTHLY REVIEW

JOURNAL WORK

This month, journal on some of the things that may have arisen while creating your tree of life. You can use the questions below as a guide to help unlock any insights you may have **discovered.**

What memories came up while drawing your tree?

....

....

Were there any people, places or experiences from the past that you had not thought about in a while?

....

....

Did any memory or feeling stand out?

....

....

Was any area of your tree unsupported or, perhaps, did you have more fruit falling than you have growing?

....

....

Is anyone or anything missing from your drawing? Why did you leave them out?

....

....

What do you feel about this tree as a whole?

....

....

How do you think this might relate to your creativity?

....

....

MEDITATION

Creativity requires freedom of the mind. This month's meditation is a form of hypnosis relaxation which will help you boost your creativity easily and effortlessly. You can find it at Month 6 at www.andreahayes.ie. Often when we are daydreaming new creative ideas take shape and grow. Make sure to listen in everyday to help you become your new creative self.

My Journal Extract

I am sitting in this lovely, quiet prayer room in Gonzaga College while I take this time to journal about our morning of art exploration. We had to choose our tools and simply express ourselves in a creative way. I resisted it at first and really felt it was a little time wasting, then something happened – I got into it. I didn't go for paint, taking a more simple approach with a packet of felt-tip pens and some white paper. I had no idea what to draw. I wanted it to be abstract so, after my initial resistance, I just got into it and somehow relaxed. All my tensions and stresses seemed to quietly lift away as I coloured in square-shaped blocks of colour. Interestingly, I was feeling very tired and hungry before I started the task, and maybe that was part of my initial opposition, then by the end I noticed I had totally switched mindset. I made the breakthrough realisation that when I feel inspired it gives me energy. It is such a contradiction but my reason to resist it at first was because I was tired, yet when I was finished my art piece I felt totally inspired and light.

I actually finished the task with a great sense of gratitude. I suddenly felt very lucky that I live in a country and a world that affords me an opportunity to express myself freely and an opportunity to enjoy free will and make my own decisions. This feeling of gratitude is growing and I am suddenly so thankful now for my hands which allowed me to draw and my mind for creating such a unique picture. I am so grateful for all the people who are facilitating this weekend retreat. This feeling of gratitude and inspiration is fuelling me to discover more about my own spiritual path. I felt something was guiding my art and I feel in a similar way that something is guiding me to become an open vessel and fill up with all this wisdom that I feel inspired to research and learn more about.

As I write now, I keep thinking of the mantra 'My wisdom will direct you' – it is going over and over in my mind and I feel like I want to surrender all control over what the outcome of anything will be and just be guided by my heart. It was sort of that way earlier with the art – I just suspended judgement after a while and got into it, and somehow it seems to have unlocked this sense of purpose in me.

I feel guided to trust the Higher Power that I am on the right path, instead of judging. I am surrendering just as I did earlier and whatever unfolds, I know it will fill me with energy and nourishment.

Speaking of which, I think I will break for lunch now. Feeling really creative and pretty amazing!

What a tonic.

Love and light,

A xx

My Journal

'It is in our darkest moments that we
must focus to see the light.'
— Aristotle

'I WISH I COULD SHOW YOU, WHEN YOU ARE **LONELY** OR IN **DARKNESS**, THE **ASTONISHING LIGHT** OF YOUR **OWN BEING**.'

– Hafiz of Shiraz

MONTH 7

Ignite Your Light

'THERE IS A **CRACK IN EVERYTHING,** THAT'S HOW THE **LIGHT GETS IN**.'

– Leonard Cohen

By now you should be starting to feel the radiance of the new version of you that is emerging. At this point in my own journey I started to accept myself fully (cracks and all), and I felt a little brighter and I seemed to have an inner glow or spark that was undeniable. However, I was also thinking a lot about my purpose. We all strive so hard to build a life that we actually enjoy waking up to each morning, but I wondered if I was missing the mark, or even the spark, in my life. During my own exploration of a deeper connection to my mind, body and soul, I became very drawn to the concept of light and I spent a long time journaling about what really lights me up.

If you embrace your desires and explore what you truly want from life, then you will be illuminated and you will find what it is that lights you up. All I needed to do was step into my light.

Over the years in work, the camera operator would often say while filming, 'Find your light.' I heard this time and time again. In TV you need to learn to see that light and how the camera sees it. It is important in all forms of photography, cinema and TV work, as your key light serves to highlight the form and dimensions of the subject in the best possible way.

It was always something I struggled with. Some of my co-hosts over the years, like my good friend Conor Clear, just seemed to instinctively find their light, but I could never quite get into mine.

So how do you find this elusive light?

Light is the natural agent that stimulates sight and makes things visible. In order to see yourself and what this world has to offer, you need to understand what lights you up. On this part of your journey you should be starting to view yourself through a new lens. We have worked through the shadow side of our personalities and now that we have embraced that darkness, we can truly burn bright and illuminate our paths ahead.

Making it your intention to love, honour and support yourself has become your recent full-time passion. You have made a commitment to not allow the daily grind of life to dim your glow – in fact, you are just starting to sparkle and shine – and this stop on our path is all about finding what lights you up and truly stepping into your light.

I must admit, I struggled with this. One of the greatest truths about having balance in your mind, body and soul is that it all must happen from the inside out. We are affected by what goes on inside – our emotions, feelings, beliefs and thoughts all in turn affect our actions, the words we speak and how we choose to experience the world. I felt I needed to simply turn on my inner light and help it to burn bright.

This was a bit harder than expected because I wasn't prepared for what I was about to discover. When you look at yourself without judgement or expectation and see yourself through unfiltered eyes, you can rediscover all of the authentic parts of your personality that may have been overlooked, silenced or neglected.

Over the past few years, I have manifested so much into my life that I once considered to be way out of my reach both professionally and personally. Health wise, I have experienced what I consider to be miracles, and outcomes to situations that I never thought possible became my reality. So it was difficult to admit that all of this wonderful abundance wasn't fulfilling me; being truly in my light was guiding me in a new direction.

But somehow, I felt a little spark to take another path and explore something different. Sometimes that calling into the light is something that is just a whisper to you at first. Often it is when you quiet down your mind, body and soul in self-reflection and meditation that you will hear that tiny voice of your authentic truth.

'Work at being in love with the person in the mirror who has been through so much but is still standing.'

– Unknown

When that little spark of truth ignites, it can shine a light on many parts of your life. You may come to realise that things that you once loved don't really work for you anymore – it could be that a relationship, friendships, where you live or maybe even the job you worked so hard to obtain no longer resonates with you. And that's OK. If this new path lights you up, then you know it's the right one.

On your new path, you may have only a glimmer of light at the start, but watch out for signposts that tell you your calling is near. Look for the signs and listen to those little whispers pointing you in the right direction.

DARE OF THE DAY

Identify the signposts that may be directing you to your new calling.

You feel pulled in a certain direction, with the knowledge that this work is yours to do. What is your work?

....

....

....

You receive incredible energy and a sense of meaning from doing the work. What gives you energy?

....

....

....

Watch out for your ego, this can be attached to fear. A part of you wants to run in the other direction but follow the work you feel guided to do. What are you afraid of?

....

....

....

You have a sense of lack in your life but thinking about this work fills a gap. What would make you feel fulfilled?

....

....

....

What vision keeps showing up in your mind's eye? Is there a dream you have always had or have you always believed you would end up doing a certain type of work? What is your vision for you?

....

....

....

Forge your own path, engage your passions and follow the light to the work that you are drawn to. This could take the form of charity endeavours, or maybe there is a particular cause you are drawn to or problem in the world, like climate change or homelessness, that draws you in. Your work could be engaging in the arts, further education, spirituality, parenting, teaching, caring, gardening or writing. You will know what it is as you will feel drawn to it and have a mysterious sense that **this work is mine to do**.

When you are clear about this, it feels like you have your soul's blueprint. I think what can stop us from following this design for our life is our own self-judgement, or we can be too concerned about what other people will think. Be aware of your inner critic saying 'you can't do that' and 'who do you think you are'. What if you could put aside the voices of self-doubt and embrace your desires? Your passions are what light you up and it is that light that illuminates your path.

DARE OF THE WEEK

Most of us are quite clear on what we don't want. Envisioning what we *do* want is much more difficult, yet it's the most critical step in the process of achieving it. Without too much thought, write the first three things that come into your mind for each statement below.

What I want:

1. ....

2. ....

3. ....

What I don't want:

1. ....

2. ....

3. ....

What moves me closer to what I want:

1. ....

2. ....

3. ....

For the next week, try to do things that will move you closer to what you want. And try to give less time to what is taking you away from achieving this dream.

It can be frustrating to be told to 'just follow your passion' when you are not sure exactly what it is that fires you up. It is so easy to lose the connection with your inner fire. So the first thing to do each day this week is set the intention that **you can and will find your passion** and step into your light.

If you're convinced that finding your passion is too hard, you'll remain closed to possibilities. You'll block the little nudges and signals that guide us all. Choose to adopt the perspective that you **can** do what you love with your life.

Every day, ask yourself, 'What is it that I love now that will ignite my light?'

If you want to contribute your passion to society and make an income from it, you need to be realistic about whether it could actually become a career. This might require some guidance from a professional.

Think about whether you would enjoy doing the activity every day. Sometimes it's good to have a passion just for fun, and turning it into work could change it from a 'love to do' to a 'have to do'.

DARE OF THE MONTH

I tried to help myself along the path to finding my passion by following a **ten-step challenge** to do things to ignite my inner spark so I could fan the flame of my light. Each day I would purposefully follow the day's intention and journal about it that night. It is harder than it might seem, and it requires time and attention, but it's worth it – just wait for the **lightbulb** breakthroughs.

These ten intentions are to push you out of your comfort zone. You can complete them at your own pace – I did them over a number of weeks. Some felt easy while others were challenging. For the next month, **use your journal to record each experience**.

It is all about finding what makes you spark and by doing the work, you will reprioritise **you**. It might be that, through exploring these intentions, you fall in love with an activity that engrosses you – something that lights you up and makes your heart sing.

1. I intend to **connect with my deeper self through creative activities that refuel my energy**. I will think back on my life and remind myself of the things I enjoyed doing, what that inner child wanted to be. I will remember the talents I developed naturally, the games I played, the books I read and see how they may apply to my life and career today. Can I capture anything from my past to help guide me towards my light?

_____

_____

_____

_____

_____

2. I intend to **explore work that is engaging and meaningful to me on a deeper level**. I will seek out people who are working in jobs they are passionate about. I will try to arrange to talk to them, email them or read about them and their careers and find out how they followed their passion for success.

_____

_____

_____

_____

_____

_____

3. I intend to **do something new that I have always wanted to do** – I will expand my comfort zone. I will not make excuses and I will follow my instinct with passion and great expectations.

4. I intend to **take time for quiet meditation and reflection** to nurture my soul. I will purposely take time to connect with nature and absorb all its beauty. I will take pictures of my journey and also spent quiet time in nature, engaging in mindful breathing and contemplation.

5. I intend to connect with my body through my favourite exercise routine. It may have been a long time since I exercised but I am willing to **try three new things to see if I can raise my heartrate** and release my body's natural endorphins.

_____

_____

_____

_____

_____

_____

6. I intend to cease my self-limiting beliefs. I will consciously **write a list of all the things I think I can't do or can't achieve and burn it**. Then on the page below replace the list with positive, encouraging and motivational **I can** statements.

_____

_____

_____

_____

_____

_____

7. I intend to embrace and **explore my personal power and my sexuality** by communicating my desires with my partner in an honest and revealing way *or* by deciding what I am seeking in a fulfilling relationship.

8. I intend to **shed my life of unnecessary obligations and unneeded possessions** by creating a home that is comfortable and beautiful and reflective of who I am. I will take time to take stock and declutter if required.

9. I intend to **live boldly, laugh loudly and get out into the world more** by engaging with new people and groups. I will bravely put myself out there more fully and completely.

10. I intend to **free myself from any rigid thoughts that keep me stuck in my professional life**. I will actively seek out new opportunities that promote learning and growth.

'F.L.Y.
First love yourself'

– Unknown

'OUR
INTENTION CREATES
OUR
REALITY.'
– Wayne Dyer

A-HA MOMENTS

When people think about Sir Isaac Newton, they think the apple falling was enough to give him the idea for his theory of gravity, but the untold part of that story is his obsession with gravitational forces prior to that lightbulb moment. Without all the work he did beforehand, the apple falling from the tree would probably not have sparked his creativity.

When those moments happened for me, it literally filled me with energy. I was on fire, I was burning bright like a star, but, just like the energy of a star, that light can quickly fade so you have to act in the moment before it shoots away.

Seize the day!

These moments often come with a burst of euphoria, and you need to capture your idea, insight or vision quickly and without question. Don't try to analyse it – just write it in your journal. I have sometimes lost the thread of a great lightbulb breakthrough and it was gone like the wind. Don't lose momentum. Within the first few hours of writing down your lightbulb idea, you need to work on it and reflect on what insights it holds for you. Lightbulb moments happen at odd times so you may need to burn the midnight oil in order to put some context around what meaning it holds for you. In other words, if you feel galvanised to take action then follow your instincts.

Turn your dream into a reality. Take action and do whatever research or additional work is required to follow your insight or idea. Maintain your momentum. Stay in your alignment. Be present with the idea and focus on the highest outcome for your greatest good. This insight showed up for you for a reason. You're here for a reason. You know it. You can feel it. Follow that dream.

'Many of life's failures are people who did not realise **how close they were to success** when they gave up.'

– Thomas A. Edison

JOURNAL WORK

Using your journal will really help you during your time of self-reflection. Allow your writing to illuminate the answers that already lie within you.

Daily journaling can allow you to explore your deepest desires and darkest secrets and connect with the passions that are waiting to be ignited. Consider the following **soul questions**.

What am I passionate about?

What lights me up?

What do I want?

What do I not want?

What has been my lightbulb breakthrough?

....

....

....

....

What dream do I need to turn into a reality?

....

....

....

....

MEDITATION

For Month 7, tune into the meditation about finding your light and igniting your passion and purpose – it can be used as a useful relaxation to inspire some lightbulb moments. You can find this meditation at www.andreahayes.ie.

My Journal Extract

Today, journal, I am feeling a little unsure – I am going to journal with my soul. I am feeling a little uncertain whether I belong in my spiritual-director course. Am I good enough? Am I being judged? Who am I to think I can do this?

I need to know that I am coming from a place of love and not ego. I am trying to name the feeling and explore the true essence of it and see if it is bringing me in the right direction.

As I sit here in silence writing every so often I am feeling a new soul awareness. I am acknowledging my feelings – naming them and then bringing them gently to the pages of this journal.

What do I desire? Desire ignites the passion to light the way to my calling. I have a strong desire to learn more about this course, and when I come from a loving place and listen and see everything through love, only more love can grow.

What do I want? I keep repeating 'thy kingdom come in me'.

What messages are you trying to tell me? My reality is viewed through my own consciousness, and as I become more aware of me, I need to trust this new reality I am creating. My ego is the one who questions, doubts and tries to stop the process.

Lightbulb insight? I am being guided to look to nature, getting rid of the old, welcoming the new – rejuvenation.

Am I inspired? I am feeling so inspired and I know this is a journey that I need to take, not worrying about where it is leading but just trusting the feelings along the way, listening to the soft, gentle whispers to my soul. It will never be a roar pushing me. I need to silence the inner critic, continue to gently fan the flames, have patience and soon my fire will burn bright and light up my life.

A x

My Journal

'Hope is being able to see that there is light despite all of the darkness.'
— Desmond Tutu

'IF YOU WANT TO FIND THE SECRETS OF THE UNIVERSE, THINK IN TERMS OF ENERGY, FREQUENCY AND VIBRATION.'

– Nikola Tesla

MONTH 8

Your Vibe Attracts Your Tribe

'EVERY HUMAN BRAIN IS BOTH A BROADCASTING AND RECEIVING STATION FOR THE VIBRATION OF THOUGHT.'

– Napoleon Hill

Is there something that connects us all? Humans across the world may actually be communicating through the same universal language and it might surprise you that it doesn't have words! In fact, we can often understand what is being conveyed before any words are spoken. No matter what language we speak, no matter what country we are from, we can all understand so much through the non-verbal language of energy and vibration. It's this invisible energy that we all carry within us that sends out magical, unseen signals about our core intentions that others can usually sense. They might not always believe or trust those instinctive interpretations but they are picking the signals up all the time.

Have you ever heard people say, 'I can read between the lines' or 'I could pick up the vibes the minute I walked into the room'? What they are feeling is energy. The vibrational energy you get from other people can often speak volumes, even before they open their mouths to say a single word!

The language of energy transcends race, culture, religion and gender. Getting a 'vibe' is often immediate; it can be felt without touch; it's invisible. Many cultures honour this energy as life force. In Chinese medicine it's called chi, a vitality that's essential to health.

From an energy standpoint, vibes is shorthand for vibrations. Many people believe that all we are is energy. We are made up of vibrating energy that draws similar vibrations to it. Energy precedes all physical manifestations, so everything that manifests itself in your life is there because it matches your vibrations. When you connect the vibration of your true, authentic self to your powerful energy source you can manifest great abundance or great scarcity – it depends on what is in harmony with your dominant vibration.

In a world that is so consumed with measuring success, measuring wealth, measuring likes, measuring friends and even measuring calories, I think measuring vibrations can be more effective than all of the above. When we choose to live our lives at a higher vibration, we are more able to stay in that positive energy flow. In this space we create a momentum where everything we want to attract is there, everything we ask for is given and, in simple terms, everything seems to go our way. When you are aware of how to stay in your true flow you can harness this energy.

For example, when you are in the flow of showing kindness or gratitude, the high vibration of your actions often leads to a flow of greater kindness coming to you and you reap the rewards of your generous, grateful, natural vibe.

This might seem difficult to learn but I promise you it is not. It is quite the opposite. You may even have been acutely aware of reading energy vibes all your life.

Have you noticed that you can take an instant like or dislike to someone? This is you picking up on that person's energy instantly and knowing it will not flow with your own. Or have you ever entered a house and instantly felt at home and comfortable or totally uneasy and nervous? You can't explain why – it's just a feeling you get based on the atmosphere. Trusting that feeling and reading the vibes is an enormously helpful clue as to whether a person, activity or place is an energy booster or energy deflator.

DARE OF THE DAY

Ask yourself before you start your day, 'What energy do I want to attract today?'

When you are aware of your inner state, it is easy to match that energy and create a flow of what you want to attract – peace, love, success, wealth, health, happiness, joy, fun. Be the energy you want to attract. It is very easy to calibrate your energy to a level that attracts what you desire. The first things to be aware of are your negative thoughts and negative beliefs. Start by eliminating them and this will immediately help change your energy.

Ask yourself:
How is my energy field? How am I feeling emotionally right now? Is my energy communicating positive or negative vibes?

Think about when you are already late and you hit a red traffic light – it can often lead to a domino effect where every light is red from then on and then you can't find parking – you attract more bad energy and before long you are having a bad day.

If you are feeling negative, ask yourself how you can change this emotion into a positive one and switch up your vibration so you are attracting the positive energy you want. If you want to feel love, think loving thoughts. A quick way to change the energy is to think of three ways you have love in your life. Choose the energy you want to attract and think of ways you already harness that vibe right now.

success LOVE health
JOY wealth FUN
PEACE happiness

I have _____ in my life because

_____

_____

_____

_____

_____

_____

Your vibe is a clue to the challenges within you that you may need to fix or address. This can be tricky for people, as we often don't even know what we are truly feeling, and we don't know how our energy is aligning itself with those feelings and vibes. The first thing is to truthfully acknowledge what your own energy level is like. Then we can truly allow the flow of energy to formulate patterns that will reveal that vibration: it will either be enhancing your life or creating blocks for you.

I became fascinated with the cause and effect of energy and how matching your vibrational energy with things, people and situations you want in your life can often quickly attract them. So the big question is how do you match your vibrational energy to that which you desire to manifest in your life?

One of the simple things you can do is make it your intention to authentically raise your energy vibe.

DARE OF THE WEEK

Try to follow the steps below with intention for a week and see how these simple strategies can boost your energy flow.

1. Wake-up intention

Every day start your morning by waking up on purpose. Start by asking yourself before your feet hit the ground, **'How do I want to feel today?'** For example, if it is **happy,** then you need to take a moment after waking to sit, breathe and think of three things that make you happy. Repeat the process with three things that make you feel other positive emotions such as success, joy, love and so on.

Starting your day with the intent of feeling a certain emotion will kick start your energy flow to attract experiences and people into your day to match that vibration.

What is my intention today?

....

....

....

2. Never leave home without a smile

When I was younger, my mother made me bless myself with holy water before I left the house and this made me feel safe and protected throughout my day. I wanted to do something similar with my daughter and we decided to start the day by physically smiling as we left the house. It can be a little difficult to start with, as you might be feeling rushed and stressed, but the more you practise, the more you just start to smile as the front door closes, and that smile begins to raise your vibration, that joyful energy is what you emit to the world. You can spot a person by their smile – we all know that one person who will be smiling brightly when you see them, in spite of what negative things might be going on for them.

So start your day with a smile and the intent of being happy and this will set in motion the energy to attract joyful people.

My reason to smile today is:

....

....

....

3. Choose wisely

How you feel and the energy you create is your choice. **Choose** how you react to things and in turn how you see your world. So if you are stuck in traffic, instead of choosing to feel stress, choose to feel gratitude for your car to get you from A to B safely.

Choose your emotions and be the driver of them. We can have upward and downward spirals of emotion – this is well documented – and to stay in that upward flow we need to choose joyful and happy emotions instead of the downward, fearful emotions.

So even when you drop your morning coffee or are running late because of traffic, ask yourself, **can you look for the positive in this situation?** How can you raise your vibration to deal with this? For me, humour is the best resource – see the funny side of things.

I am a genuinely positive person, but of course there were times in my life when I wasn't always happy on the inside and that reflected in my reactions to things, especially when dealing with chronic pain. But you alone have to **choose** to make a **conscious** effort to look for the good in every situation.

My vibe today will be:

....

....

....

4. Stop complaining

Several key discoveries in neuroscience have changed our understanding about the brain and how we think and act.

Our ability to effectively understand our emotional energy is vital to our happiness, so when we are not in the flow of happiness we can't attract that. One of the things proven to be bad for our mood (and the mood of your family, friends and colleagues) is complaining. You might not think you complain, but I dare you to try for a day to monitor every time you complain about something. It could be something small, like your tea going cold or missing your favourite TV show, but this behaviour is bad for your mood and it's also bad for your brain and your health.

So replace complaining with love and decide to radiate **love** on purpose. Decide you want love to be your dominant flowing energy, allow it to permeate your daily thoughts and actions with light and watch how the flow changes. Instead of the harsh, forceful energy of complaining, this energy is more soothing, uplifting and gentle. Actively spend time every day sending out waves of love and watch the tidal flow of energy that you attract.

No complaining – my reason to be grateful is:

....

....

....

5. Cosmic ordering

I like to call this online shopping from the Universe. Take some time this week to reflect on what you really want in your life. **Write down** what you want, with as much detail as possible, in your journal – you can make it into a shopping list if there is more than one thing. Then match what you have written down with the **vibe** you need to emit to manifest the thing you want. For example, say you want a new dream job. Your vibe might be confident, grateful or proud of this achievement. Your energy will begin to flow with those vibes to begin the process to manifest your wish.

My cosmic wish is:

....

....

....

Next, start **visualising**. Take your dream job into reality by allowing your mind to daydream what it would really feel like to have that job. This is an important part of the vibrational alignment. You need to feel the vibration of manifesting your goal in every part of your being. Creative visualisation helps the subconscious mind to believe what you are imagining is really true. Live the dream in your mind in detail. The more clearly you can visualise it, the quicker you will bring your energy into alignment with your desire. Repeat this process for a whole week, daydreaming and living the dream in your mind every day before you get up or before you go to sleep.

When you have the image very clear in your mind, the next thing is to **add on** how you will **feel** if what you desire manifested. You must really feel as if the dream has come true – allow that sensation to flow from head to toe, and your vibration will attract that energy quicker! Feelings are the most powerful vibration lifters. You can think about it and talk about it, but unless you **feel** it, you won't raise your vibrational flow.

Then **end with gratitude**. Imagine being so grateful for your perfect job – fill your whole body with this feeling of gratitude and imagine saying thank you to your new boss for hiring you.

I often play a game where I write a **thank-you letter** for what it is I want to attract on one side of a page, and I notice as I am writing that my gratitude expands and I am tricking my mind into believing what I desire is already there. Then on the other side of the page I write what I am already thankful for. I include everything I feel blessed to have right now. This positive energy of gratitude raises your vibration to a higher state.

If you can practise this for a week, or even for the next month, it will become easy and you can almost start manifesting on command.

Your vibe attracts your tribe.

This saying has always resonated with me, but it seemed to have more meaning after studying the power of neuroscience. As we have discovered, at a basic level, we are all energy, and energy has power, positive and negative. **Like literally attracts like.** So if you have a happy outlook, you will attract happy friends into your life! And you must remember that you have to be true to your authentic self. If you are pretending to be someone that you're not, you're going to attract a tribe that has nothing in common with the real you. It's a chain reaction. If you are a genuinely positive individual, your energy or vibration will attract other genuinely positive individuals. But if you are just 'trying' to be positive and not truly embodying the emotion, your energy or vibration will attract others vibrating at a similar frequency. You need to be yourself to truly attract likeminded souls.

For example, some people just radiate positive energy and when you meet them you just instantly 'click' and you want to be around them; you feel good in their presence. Why is that? It is because their energy is communicating to your energy, their vibe is in line with your flow, you are cultivating the same energy field.

We don't attract what we want, we attract who we are.

Your emotional energy is precious and needs to be protected. You need to become aware of energy depletion. When you see that your energy is becoming low, you need to locate the source of the leak. As with a car, a small leak can sometimes become a major problem, followed by an overheated engine. And when your engine overheats, you breakdown. Similarly, the people around us can break us down or elevate us!

Many years ago, a magazine article categorised people into two groups – radiators and drains. This concept was popularised by Oprah Winfrey, who once, when asked what she wished she'd learned earlier in life, said, 'I wish I'd known how to distinguish radiators from drains.' Learning that lesson can make the difference between a toxic and a healthy relationship.

Dear ....

....

....

....

....

....

....

....

....

....

....

....

....

....

Signed: ....

'*Radiators* beam warmth, kindness, love, happiness and enthusiasm. They smile when you walk into a room, are genuinely interested in others and make you feel good about yourself. Radiators bring out the very best in people. **DRAINS** have a more negative outlook on life and their glass is always half-empty. They can be self-absorbed, demanding and will often take-take-take without ever giving anything back. Drains zap your energy levels with their constant need for reassurance and leave you feeling totally diminished. Drains are toxic.'

– Oprah Winfrey

DARE OF THE MONTH

You'll recognise **radiators** instantly because each time you're in their company you come away feeling great about yourself and the world. These people know how to listen. They hold a space for us while we talk – they are never simply waiting to talk themselves. Radiators motivate us to succeed in life, encourage us to drive towards our goals and support us, whatever our chosen journey may hold. Importantly, radiators are happy for us when we're happy – there is no envy, jealousy or resentment.

For the next month, **be mindful of who the radiators are in your world.**

Drains are quite simply draining to be around – they literally drain us of our energy. They can be very toxic with their thoughts and words and are often negative about everything. We feel worse about the world and the people in it after spending time in their company. These are the people who don't listen. They only view the world through their own eyes and they don't care about your world. Drains will continue to ask for your time and your resources while rarely offering anything back. A drain can be someone who affects your confidence, momentum and flow – it is often the 'friend' who brings you down.

For the next month, **think about who the drains are in your world.**

You should also be aware of **online drains** who take to social media to complain. They can post negative comments or pull you up for bad grammar. They will ask you to retweet their blog post but are slow to like or support your posts. They see another's success as their failure.

Online drains:

....

....

Instead, gravitate towards **online radiators**. They will post positive things that resonate with you. They respond positively to good news and are generous with their likes, shares, mentions and virtual happy faces. They are engaging, genuine and make cyberspace a nicer place to be.

Online radiators:

....

....

EXCEPTIONS

Of course, there are exceptions that we can't avoid, like certain **family members** that are part of our lives, that may seem to have completely opposite energy to ours and can cause major sparks. See those people as teachers and instead send them unconditional love – but take a cautious approach to the amount of time you spend with them. Set healthy boundaries and stick to them.

What if you have a problem in **work**? It can be difficult to navigate the office environment with **co-workers** who have all the tell-tale signs of being a drain. This is a learning opportunity too. Set the tone and keep it professional – don't allow them to zap your energy by offloading their personal misery, anger and frustration on you; keep the conversation and interactions all about work.

Family and work drains:

....

....

....

RECURRING PATTERNS

Unless you stop and begin to examine who you are attracting in your life, you will keep the flow the same. This familiar pattern will continue and you will attract the same types of people and situations into your life over and over.

What am I attracting?

....

....

....

> Positivity attracts positivity and negativity attracts
> negativity. Each energy feeds off each other.

What do I want to attract?

....

....

....

'POSITIVE THINKING
is more than just a tagline.
It changes the way we behave.
And I firmly believe that when
I am positive, it not only makes
me better, but it also makes
those around me better.'

– Harvey Mackay

MONTHLY REVIEW

JOURNAL WORK

Here are some **soul questions** for Month 8.

1. How do I want to **feel** today?

2. Who are the radiators in my world?

3. Who are the drains in my world?

4. Social media audit: can I review my online tribe?

5. We don't attract what we want; we attract who we are. What am I attracting and why?

_____

_____

_____

_____

_____

6. How would I describe my vibe?

_____

_____

_____

_____

_____

MEDITATION

This month's guided meditation will take you on a journey that will focus on ways to increase your positive energy by raising your vibration to the highest level so you can attract the people and situations you want into your life. When we meditate we naturally plug into our own unique vibe and this helps us open up to all the good life has to offer. You'll find it under Month 8 at www.andreahayes.ie.

'DO SOMETHING TODAY
THAT YOUR
FUTURE SELF
WILL THANK YOU
FOR.'

– Unknown

My Journal Extract

As the summer comes to an end, I feel it is an ending of sorts for me too. September is a time of mini renewal in many ways – as Brooke prepares to go back to school, I am preparing to start a new chapter in my mindset. I have had a lot of time to digest all the losses and miscarriages we have endured in the last year and I am asking myself if I have done anything to attract that energy of loss – maybe after the first one, I had an expectation of more loss – so I feel I need to totally switch up my thinking and attitude towards my fertility. I had a meeting with the fertility clinic and the news that my egg quantity and quality are both low is very negative news too, but I just feel I need to cling onto hope.

I have considered the idea of a donor egg and I just do not feel it is for me at this time. My heart is telling me to remain positive and hopeful so, in order to be in that space, I need to remove the fear of loss which, subconsciously, since the complete molar pregnancy, I have been carrying around. I needed to go through the emotions of grieving and now it is time for me to move forward with abundant, fertile thoughts. I know it is easier said than done but I need to give it a try and I am willing to make it my intention and switch up my thinking.

I am aware that old fear-based feelings will resurface and when they do I will not fight them but acknowledge them and say that might have been the case in the past but it is not the case for me now – loss is past: I feel health, fertility and a healthy baby will prevail.

I have to see the blessing in experiencing the losses, they have taught me so much about the miracle of life and the precious gift a child is to any family. I feel that writing honestly about my feelings of fear, loss, sadness and total hopelessness has allowed me to heal and move to this place of peace and hope.

A x

'When I started counting my blessings, my whole life turned around.'

– Willie Nelson

My Journal

'Ego says, "Once everything falls into
place I'll feel peace." Spirit says, "Find
peace and then everything will fall
into place".
— Marianne Williamson

'Flying starts from the ground. The more grounded you are, the higher you fly.'

– J.R. Rim

MONTH 9

Plug in: Grounding, Centring and Rooting

'THE ULTIMATE CONNECTION IS WHEN YOU ARE CONNECTED TO THE CREATOR OF THE UNIVERSE.'

– Joel Osteen

The word **grounded** always seems to come up whenever I have discussions about positive mental health. How often have you been told to 'centre' yourself before a big interview or meeting? Or have you been told that someone is very stable because of their upbringing and strong family 'roots'. Certainly among my spiritually inclined friends, the concepts of being grounded and being centred are very important.

Most people don't question what this means – somehow we all seem to know that the term means that a person is 'down to earth', 'balanced', 'sound'. Some might even say they are 'going back to their roots' when describing a positive return to a situation, relationship or place in life.

Do you feel mentally **grounded**?

Is your body **rooted** in your being?

Are you **centred** with your true, authentic self?

What does it truly mean anyway?

The basic meaning of **grounded** is to connect to the earth. It's a verb (to ground through the feet) and an adjective (a grounded feeling). Not surprisingly, it comes from the process of electricity – electrically connecting to the earth itself is often called **earthing** or **grounding**.

Electrical grounding is an essential part of everyday life. The many electrical appliances and devices we use every day (computers, televisions, microwave ovens and so on) generate lots of 'noise' (disturbance in the electrical signals) that can damage equipment or cause it to work less efficiently. This concept got me thinking.

After trying so hard to understand my own energy flow, vibration and the momentum of this energy, I wondered if perhaps I wasn't grounded – was it possible that the noise and distractions in my life were preventing me from harnessing this energy I worked so hard to attract? By not being centred, rooted and grounded, could I be missing opportunities?

When I looked at my life, I had to acknowledge that there was a lot of noise. Often there were so many things fighting for my attention each day that I felt I was being pulled in many directions. The biggest culprit for me was the constant social media at my fingertips. So despite my best efforts, it seemed that I was becoming ungrounded a lot more often than I would like to admit.

To be truly happy with where you are in life right now, it is important to feel grounded, rooted and centred in your mind, body and soul. When you truly stand in your power, you instantly give yourself a launching pad to fly from.

Creating a sense of grounding in your life is really about taking responsibility for what is showing up in your light right now. It is so important to take responsibility for your world and to understand that we take any internal stress and turmoil with us until we learn to deal with it, so if we are rooted in drama, that very chaos will keep coming with us to the next place.

But what does it mean to be grounded? Being grounded is being firmly rooted within our self and in reality. To be grounded is the ability to maintain balance, stability and presence of mind, no matter what is happening around you.

Being ungrounded is the opposite – I call it being distracted, lost, anxious and untethered – and it seems to me that being ungrounded is a worldwide epidemic, especially with our youth.

DARE OF THE DAY

As you go through your day, make it your intention to notice if you are grounded and also become aware of what triggers you to become unbalanced and not centred in your source energy. Use your journal to write about your experience.

I feel grounded when:

....

....

....

....

I feel ungrounded when:

....

....

....

....

....

Signs you could use some grounding:

1. You have lots of great inspiration, but you can't seem to ground it and get projects finished, or you lose focus and the momentum to complete them.

2. You have lost a bit of your get-up-and-go. Your mind wants to complete a task but your body isn't working with that vision – it's almost like you are off centre. You might feel nervous or a little spaced out with no inclination to move forward.

3. You have a lot of internal chatter in your mind, or you are spending a good deal of time daydreaming or questioning things more than usual. This isn't a bad thing, but you need to get these new concepts rooted into your life so you can make changes or implement your new ideas.

4. You are anxious about change, but you are finding it difficult to communicate how you are feeling. You might wish to feel safe – often this manifests in an impulse to hold onto how things are. And you might be hoarding things or be unwilling to spend money because you feel worried about the future.

5. If you have a strong urge to either stay inside or be physical and go outside, again you are not in balance – or your inner voice might be trying to tell you that you need to get outside to root yourself in nature to gain clarity.

When you are well grounded you have the following traits:

* good self-esteem,

* excellent confidence,

* unmoved by other people's dramas,

* unshakable moral compass,

* unshakable spiritual convictions,

* awareness of your worth,

* positive opinion of yourself,

* can't be played by people – you are too good for that,

* form your own opinions about things,

* leadership in life,

* courageous,

* respectful,

* respected for who you are,

* see right through whiners, cowards, pity-seekers and manipulators; refuse to play their game of lies.

I can become more grounded by:

....

....

....

....

....

'It was when I stopped
searching for home
within others and
lifted the foundations
of home within myself
I found there were no
roots more intimate
than those between a
mind and body that have
decided to be whole.'

– Rupi Kaur

For me, in my quest to heal myself, I have done a lot of research into this whole area. From a scientific perspective, the idea is that the earth has a mild negative charge. Over time, especially in modern life, our bodies build up a positive charge. Direct contact with the earth can even out this positive charge and return the body to a neutral state.

Many people don't have this contact with the earth anymore, and some experts wonder if this is a contributor to the (many) rising health problems we face today. The theory is that this build-up of positive charge over time can lead to health problems. So grounding, earthing and centring could have physical wellness benefits as well as mental and spiritual rewards.

By consciously practising becoming grounded, we are able to more frequently move to this state. Like almost everything, the more you do it, the easier it becomes. When we are grounded, we are 'in the flow' and 'connected'. This is our natural state and it is where we can most effectively create and attract the results we want in our lives. It is from this place of being grounded that we operate most effectively and therefore are optimised for success in any endeavour.

Grounding can help you to:

* reduce stress, lethargy and a lack of motivation,
* increase your emotional and mental health,
* bring clarity to your life path and purpose,
* know your own wisdom, thoughts, beliefs and desires,
* grow stronger and taller in all areas,
* bring understanding to your situation,
* reduce feelings of chaos, clutter and indecision,
* take responsibility for where you are currently.

DARE OF THE WEEK

This week, try to become aware of what triggers your energy to become ungrounded. When you find yourself around someone, maybe in the workplace or within the family, who always brings drama and negative energy to the environment, do you find yourself getting sucked in? Maybe these types of people trigger your frustration, anger or anxiety.

For the next seven days, become aware of what is triggering you – try to write about a person or situation that shifted your energy in your day. These triggers can come from anywhere in your external world – shopping, social media, traffic jams, relationships in love and work, finances and so on.

Be aware of situations or people that make you feel anxious or unstable, as these are often responsible for stealing our energy. Being grounded allows us to preserve our energy instead of giving it all away.

What are my triggers this week?
Monday:

Tuesday:

Wednesday:

Thursday:

Friday:

Saturday:

....

....

Sunday:

....

....

So how can you become grounded, centred and rooted so you are in flow every day? What I have learned is that you don't have to be a reiki master to bring life-force energy into your everyday life – I have studied many healing modalities and went to many wonderful healers, but I discovered the best person to bring balance and grounding is yourself.

Whenever you feel misaligned it is easy to get back in flow with the universal life energy. You can tap into a constant energetic powerhouse by using certain techniques to ground, heal and balance your energy levels – just as a professional energy healer would restore and balance you.

I have outlined some of the most helpful tools I use below but, like all things, to make it a habit, you need to practise.

DARE OF THE MONTH

This month, make a conscious intention to ground, centre and root your energy. You can take one of the areas below per week and then recap all three in the last week, or do them whenever you feel you need to as the month goes by. The important thing is to read and absorb the exercises below and practise them.

For me, grounding myself is a mechanism that I put into practice on three levels: mind, body and soul. This doesn't need to be a harsh process, but rather one that aligns, so this month focus on these affirmations.

MIND:

I stabilise and ground
my mental energies.

BODY:

I firmly focus my body in the present
moment and root myself into that space.

SOUL:

I centre my soul and spirit to my heart
energy and my true, authentic self.

'Walk as if you are
kissing the Earth
with your feet.'

– Thich Nhat Hanh

1. Grounding the Mind

Throughout the day, try to check in with your consciousness. Is your awareness in your body or are you in your head and are your thoughts racing?

* Become aware of where you are and what you are doing.

* Become aware of your thoughts.

* Bring your thoughts into the present and state whatever you are doing
  – for example, 'Right now I am walking the dog' or 'Right now I am
  present.'

If you feel ungrounded or anxious, focus your energy on your feet. Bring all of your consciousness to your feet, wiggle your toes, feel your connection to the Earth and command yourself to ground.

* I command my energy fields to align and be brought back into balance
  and for me to ground fully into the present moment.

* I am aware. I am alert. I am conscious. I am present. I am here now.

2. Rooting the Body

During this month, try to imagine yourself just like a tree, and in doing so you must acknowledge that, as a tree, you grow both upward and downward. We are more familiar with going forward, moving up, growing up, waking up or ascending higher rather than shifting our focus on our energy rooting downward – nobody wants to move *down* in the world?

Try to think like a tree – imagine you have strong, healthy roots. Try to feel the energy of creation moving downward through you, and envision a cord rooting to the ground, connecting you with the earth's centre.

Make a conscious effort throughout the month to walk with that focus. Try walking slowly, being mindful of each step you take. Feel the ground beneath you. This is best done outside in nature, barefoot if possible, but don't use that as an excuse – you can really do it anywhere, in any weather, with any footwear.

'At the centre
of your being
**you have
the answer**;
you know who
you are and
you know what
you want.'

– Lao Tzu

3. Centring the Soul

This month, as you focus on centring yourself, you might start to see how some people have the effect of moving you off-centre. You'll notice that moods are 'contagious', and the people you spend time with have a profound effect on you, your energy and your mindset. So this month, try to protect your soul energy from the effects of negative people and their energy. Sit in silence and centre yourself with three deep, slow breaths. Imagine yourself connecting with the heart centre – you can place your hands on your heart to help with the visualisation. If you feel ungrounded from a harsh energy exchange or being around an energy drainer, you need to learn to release that energy and shield yourself.

✳ Imagine placing an energy shield around yourself by envisioning a bright light surrounding your body – this will stop negative energies from filtering into yours.

✳ Imagine a large funnel over the top of your crown, or above your heart, and see it beginning to hoover up any negative energy from people or places you might have been that day. Give the energy a colour and visualise it disappearing into the funnel, just like if you were vacuuming your house.

✳ Now imagine flooding your heart space or full body with the energy of pure, unconditional love – breathe it in and visualise it filling your whole body; you can give it a colour and see it all around you.

✳ Finally, when you are ready, imagine seeing your energy shield shining bright and keep it there as you open your eyes and continue with your day.

MONTHLY REVIEW

JOURNAL WORK

Try out these **soul questions** for month nine.

I feel mentally **grounded** ...

When?

....

....

How?

....

....

Where?

....

....

Why?

....

....

My body is **rooted** in my being ...

When?

....

....

How?

....

....

Where?

Why?

I am **centred** with my true authentic self ...

When?

How?

Where?

Why?

MEDITATION

This month's meditation is a guided visualisation to help root all your energy into the core of the earth so you are grounded, centred and plugged into your true authentic self. This meditation will also help you clear any negative energy you may have attracted and once again tune into your natural state of balance. You can find it at Month 9 at www.andreahayes.ie.

My Journal Extract

Today I was driving, and when I arrived at my destination I didn't quite remember how I got there. I stopped myself and could see that was me being ungrounded – I let my mind take me into a trace, it was classic highway hypnosis.

But what was it that got me there? Worry. I was worrying about work, I was trying to control life and push the outcome, I was in the world of illusion where my mind drifts into this fear place and I lose my footing in the now and my physical body.

I was thinking about being rooted in the here and now, and how I could stay fully present in the **now** moment – this is where our power is – and I began to think of my neighbour gardening. I pass him almost every day when I am out walking.

His garden is always in bloom regardless of the season, because he gives it attention daily. A good gardener will tend to their flowers and plants by watering them, feeding them, positioning them in the correct light and burying their roots into the soil of the earth. We never hold the plant suspended in air above the ground. It seems obvious but no matter how good of a gardener you are, if the plant is not actually rooted in the ground, it will not grow. In the same way, if I am not rooted in the realities that are within and around my world, my best plans will not grow and bloom.

So accepting where we are in life is most important – it reminds me of the saying 'bloom where you are rooted'. I need to honour my roots and ground myself and my visions in order to grow and flourish. I need to really think about this concept and do some work around it.

A x

My Journal

'A mind at peace, a mind centred and not focused on harming others, is stronger than any physical force in the universe.'

— Wayne Dyer

'The moment you *change your perception,* is the moment you *rewrite the chemistry* of your body.'

– Dr Bruce Lipton

MONTH 10

Body Talk

'Treat your body like a temple, not a woodshed.
THE MIND AND THE BODY WORK
TOGETHER. YOUR BODY NEEDS TO
BE A GOOD SUPPORT SYSTEM FOR
THE MIND AND THE SPIRIT.
If you take good care of it, your body can
take you wherever you want to go, with the
power and the strength and energy and
vitality you will need to get there.'

– Jim Rohn

I believe that in order for us to be the masters of our own true calling and destiny, we need to pay attention to the trinity of our **mind, body and soul**. This is something I work hard on each day and I feel it has brought me so much inner balance and peace.

It might surprise you to read that every day our bodies are communicating and sending messages to various cells, organs and systems to keep things functioning in a state of equilibrium. That's the goal, but sometimes we are out of balance and we need to make sure we hear the subtle messages of our bodies so we can get back to optimum health.

Think of the body as a barometer for our whole self. When we're listening, it can give us signals that will ultimately lead us to a life of happiness, fulfilment and complete wellness.

Everybody has their own idea of what it means to be well. My idea of a healthy diet might mean eating no meat and lots of fruit and veggies, while someone else will eat a low-fat diet or another person might eat lots of meat and dairy products. There is no single path when it comes to health and wellbeing. However, one thing is true for us all. In every **body** there is an incredible intelligence. When you trust this body wisdom and really listen to what your body is trying to tell you, you will be guided to what you really need and want.

BODY WISDOM

Think about the messages we take for granted every day when our body is communicating with us.

SLEEP

How do you know when it's time to go to bed? Your body tells you. The first clue might be a yawn, then your brain might think about going to bed. When we are tired our breathing changes – it becomes deeper and more subdued and we can often feel physical signs like coldness, all signalling that it's time to rest.

We often ignore the signs and try not to listen, but falling asleep is inevitable. Eventually, you will become so tired you have to sleep.

FALLING IN LOVE

Love at first sight might be a cliché, but it's undeniable that we have a physical reaction in our gut when we are attracted to someone! Some people refer to it as getting butterflies in your stomach, but whatever you want to call it, being around the person you love can cause tangible, physical reactions that are clear signs this is a good match. The same can be said about getting the opposite – watch out for those shivers down your spine when something or someone just isn't right for you.

NOURISHMENT

Every day your body tells you what it needs. A simple example of that is food. When you're hungry, physical signs can be the first indicator that you need to eat. You might notice a growling stomach; some people get a headache or light-headedness when they are thirsty. When you ignore your body's need for food, you can have a big physical reaction, like a shakiness or weakness in your body when your blood sugar goes so low it has to stop to refuel.

PAIN

Often before we are consciously aware that we have hurt ourselves, our bodies will signal danger with pain. However, you will probably have reacted involuntarily – even before you were aware of the injury. It's like pricking your finger: a reflex response occurs within the spinal cord. Motor neurons are activated and the muscles of your arm contract, moving your hand away from the sharp object. This occurs in a fraction of a second. This sudden pain is how our body communicates the warning signals for the body.

STRESS AND ANXIETY

Anxiety is not just a neurological measurement. You can experience anxiety physically as well. For example, you might feel shaky before a big presentation or meeting. Actors often say they feel sick before a performance, or you could feel restless in your sleep the night before a big interview or starting a new job or course. These experiences are both physical and emotional. Our body is trying to process something scary, unknown and overwhelming, and if the thoughts of the experience are stressful it could manifest in anxiety.

Sadly, I think, more often than not we ignore our bodies. We live in a world where pushing ourselves to the physical limit is applauded and seen as admirable. When we stay an extra few hours in the office to complete a task or continue to work through lunch or miss valuable sleep to get up early to pack everything into our busy day, it is our bodies that pay the price of our negligence while we push ourselves in order to appear successful, strong, invincible and superhuman.

I started to experience extreme exhaustion a few years ago while I was in my superhuman phase. In addition to missing all the physical signs that my chronic health condition was getting worse, I continued to push myself. I got up earlier, went to bed later and drank more caffeine and filled up on sugar to keep up with my own outlandish schedule.

I was totally ignoring my body talking to me – it was quite clearly telling me to slow down. My body was physically breaking down in every area, from increased pain, bad skin and total exhaustion to clouded thinking, and I did not do anything about it. And, importantly, no one really said a word to me about it, as it suited them that I was hitting my deadlines and delivering.

Ultimately, everything came crashing down around me. I broke down. But it wouldn't have had to be that way if I had just listened to my body. As someone with a chronic health condition, I needed to take ownership of my own role in the demise of my health – I wasn't helping myself.

'WHEN YOU ARE IN **VIBRATIONAL HARMONY,** YOUR BODY PRODUCES WHATEVER IT NEEDS TO REMAIN IN **PERFECT BALANCE'**

– Abraham Hicks

DARE OF THE DAY

Have a conversation with your body today and listen to what it is saying. Sit in silence and write down the messages your body is communicating to you through your thoughts and sensations.

My body is trying to say:

_____

_____

_____

_____

_____

_____

_____

_____

_____

The body knows what feels good to it in any given moment. The internal wisdom of your own unique body has the advantage of not only being in touch with your mind but also receiving instinctive messages from your soul and heart centre. Your body is your best tool for learning what you truly need right now.

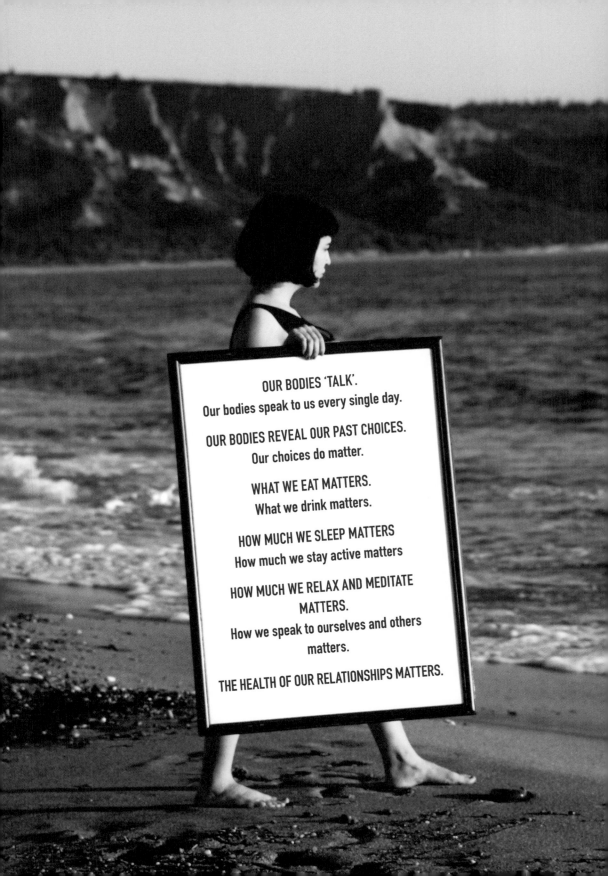

DARE OF THE WEEK

Anyone can learn to communicate better, and a great place to start is to recognise your own **serenity signals** and **alarm signals**. Learning to trust your body is like having a direct line to the best teacher or guru.

This week, as you go about your day-to-day routine, tune into your body and the little messages it tries to share. You can make a note of them in your journal. We are looking for positive (serenity) and negative (alarm) signals.

SERENITY SIGNALS

When the internal messages you receive from your body are aligned with the actions of your true, authentic self and your core values, you will likely feel at one with yourself – you will feel calm, peaceful and grounded in happiness.

For example, when I do my Bethany volunteer work, I feel very peaceful and happy for giving my time in that way. I sometimes find myself singing 'Walk in the Light' afterwards, which gives me a good signal that I am aligned in serenity.

Day:

Action:

Serenity Signal:

Feeling:

'When we're awake in
our bodies and sense,
the world comes alive.

———•———

Wisdom, creativity
and love are
discovered as we relax
and awaken through
our bodies.'

– Tara Brach

ALARM SIGNALS

When your actions are not in keeping with your true self and you reject your body's signals and take action or do something different from what you truly want to do, you will notice that you may begin to feel exhausted, overwhelmed, upset, disconnected, in pain or anxious.

For example, when I over-commit myself to projects that are not aligned with my core values, I feel exhausted and overwhelmed after a day of giving my time to the work. This tells me that this work isn't good for my body.

Day: ....

Action: ....

Alarm: ....

Feeling: ....

Are you listening to your body today?
What do you do with that information?

I found that keeping a pain journal was very helpful for me when I needed to tell my doctor about the changes in my pain. A health journal is an excellent way to become more aware of what your body is trying to communicate to you. Over time, you can reflect on periods of when you were ill or well and see if there were any tell-tale signs of what was ahead.

Unresolved emotions are one of the reasons stress, pain, anxiety and tension build up in the body. Allowing yourself to fully explore the relationship between your physical body and the manifestation of ailments and your emotional state can be a very eye-opening process.

This might be something you want to explore in more detail when reflecting on your health journal.

DARE OF THE MONTH

This month, try to tune in to your body. We are all innately intuitive and when we tune into our sensations they can reveal bigger issues in our body. I have broken the exercise down into **four parts**, so focus on each one for a week and journal about the outcome and experience.

WEEK 1: PICKING UP PHYSICAL SENSATIONS FROM YOUR BODY

If we tune into our senses on a daily basis, we can receive important messages from our body.

* **Sight:** be observant – any changes in your skin, hair or shape need to be monitored and examined.

* **Touch:** cold – frequently getting the chills when no one else is. Hot – getting hot flushes or constantly warmer than everyone else. Itchy – your skin is irritated by touch. Any of these sensation signals need to be checked out by your GP.

* **Taste:** something tastes a bit different – any unpleasant taste is a clear signal more examination is needed.

* **Hearing:** hearing something a little different in your body, like changes in your breathing or a cough that lingers for weeks or a persistent hiccup – anything you can't explain is a warning sign from the body.

* **Feeling:** notice any strong feelings – you might be exhausted despite getting a good night's sleep, or maybe you can't sleep and have a racing mind. Sometimes we feel a little spaced out and experience forgetfulness or brain fog. Your feelings matter, so any changes can be your body's way of talking to you.

I recognise my body is sending me signals and talking to me by:

....

....

....

....

WEEK 2: RECOGNISING YOUR NUMBING STRATEGIES

Sometimes we do not want to see the signs that our bodies are trying to communicate and we can often ignore our bodies' physiological signals (for example, sweaty hands, jaw clenching, stomach churning, feeling sick, dizzy or out of control). Any time your body feels tense or uncomfortable, you need to listen. However, rather than listening to these internal signals, we often use our own time-tested numbing strategies.

This week become aware of and alert to any numbing you might be doing. Often we numb ourselves to get through a difficult experience – sometimes it is the only way we can function, as the experience is too overwhelming to face. Out of fear and self-protection, we numb. It can happen in shock situations, such as a car crash or a bereavement. However, it can also happen daily as a reaction to stress, deadlines, constant pressure to perform, being too busy or just not being happy in life.

It is important to understand that the more the body numbs, the less we are present in our body, and this can cause daily experiences and feelings to be dulled and we are robbed of much of life's joy. Below are some common numbing strategies to be aware of.

* **Food, alcohol, drugs**: if we become we become numb, to the consumption of any of the above, we can self-medicate and use them as a crutch to help us sleep, relax or feel less numb or to numb us even more.

* **Addictions, self-harm, hoarding, being constantly busy, constantly consuming or any excessive or obsessive behaviour**: it is easy to become disconnected from reality by engaging in any of these behaviours. Professional help and guidance is needed to understand the exact cause of the behaviour.

* **Not living in reality, excessive emotional reactions, lying to others or yourself, blaming others for things not going well in your life**: when you become numb to your intuitive senses, many things can manifest in your life, and sometimes you project what is going on internally outward to others and start to live beyond the realm of reality. This is often an indication that you need to talk to a professional.

Denial: the numb-it-out strategy often goes hand in hand with the denial strategy. Also, sometimes we allow ourselves to go totally numb and just plaster over the problem for a short period so we can ignore it – be aware of Band-Aids like sugar fixes, alcohol and drugs to ignore the messages from our body until we are ready to do something about it.

All of the above have something in common. They don't solve the underlying problem that our bodies are trying to alert us to.

I try to numb out what is really going on by:

_____

_____

_____

_____

_____

_____

'I finally realised that being grateful to my body was key to giving more love to myself.'

– Oprah Winfrey

Tune into what you already know intuitively is good for you. I gave up following diets and reading about what should be good for me and began to do what I trusted was right for my body with food, alcohol, sleep and even social and personal commitments. Link in with your inner wisdom for the next week and do the same.

INTUITIVE EATING

Eat a healthy diet, giving up anything that no longer resonates with your inner body, imagining flooding your body with love, nutrition and wellness.

Try this simple exercise during your next meal to begin practising the art of intuitive eating.

* Prior to the meal, tune into your hunger level.

* Acknowledge and note how you are feeling going into the meal (physically, mentally and so on).

* During your meal, try to enjoy it. Chew your food thoroughly. Allow for at least twenty minutes to enjoy at least one meal a day.

* Put your fork down between bites. Check in with your hunger and fullness cues throughout.

* Stop eating if you feel full – don't feel you need to finish the plate.

Becoming mindful about how big your portions are and when you eat may change your eating habits, and you might notice you eat a little less and enjoy your food a little more.

INTUITIVE DRINKING

I am not a doctor but it's safe to say we should all drink more water, and for good reason too. Over our lifespan, our kidneys, which transport water to our tissues, gradually lose some of their efficiency. Also, nerves that signal thirst gradually decline. The combination means that you may be unaware that you're not getting adequate hydration. This is why it is so important to listen to your body. Ideally, if you sip throughout the day you won't need to hear the messages of thirst, but if you experience headaches, fatigue or brain fog it is possible your kidneys are trying to tell you to consume fluids.

One thing to watch is your **alcohol consumption**. It is good to become conscious of when it is advisable to skip that extra glass of wine. Listen to your body: a little vino now and then is fine, but try to stick to the recommended medical guidelines on alcohol servings per week. Also, remember, as we age our ability to tolerate alcohol changes – the body retains less water, so alcohol becomes more concentrated and therefore more potent.

It is all about being intuitive; a hangover is probably the biggest message the body sends to tell us we overdid things. Live and learn and ask your body if now is a good time to give up.

I plan to become more intuitive about what I consume this week by:

....

....

....

....

By this week you should be able to see, feel and identify emotions that, as you will become increasingly aware, manifest themselves physically. The body is so intelligent. Consider your slouched posture when you feel sad – your body is reacting to that emotion. Or do you get a clenched jaw and tightness when you are anxious? Becoming more aware means seeing the mind–body connection.

Being *in* your body and knowing what this feels like when you're stressed is very important. It's common to carry stress in your body in the form of tense shoulders, a stomach 'in knots', through shallow breathing or in other ways. When people carry stress in their bodies, they're often not even aware of it. A body scan meditation is a practice that can be performed daily that develops your ability to intentionally move stress from your body by moving your attention around and releasing the feelings of tension. It also teaches you to focus deeply on different regions of your body.

BODY SCAN

I have used this scanning meditation technique myself for years. It has become my bedtime ritual since I studied clinical hypnotherapy. It is a useful **grounding** exercise as it brings awareness back into balance. Not only does the body scan help to clear a cluttered mind, it is also an excellent tool in identifying physical stresses and, for me, it helped manage my chronic pain.

For me, pain can be so overwhelming in one part of my body that other imbalances are neglected. This exercise helps me take notice of how each part of my body feels, without trying to change anything. It can be difficult to get started but, as time goes by, you will find that you become more at ease and less driven by the thoughts, feelings and sensations that constantly arise within your body.

The most helpful attitude to adopt is 'relaxed curiosity'. See if you can remain open and curious about whatever comes up in your body, mind and soul. Maintain silence, deep listening – hear what your body is trying to say to you.

You might want to lie down, but you can also do it sitting up, especially if that makes it easier for you to stay awake.

1. Closing your eyes can be helpful to allow you to focus or, if you'd rather, you can always lower and half-close your eyes.

2. Bring awareness to the body, breathing in and out, noticing touch and pressure where it makes contact with the seat or floor. Throughout this practice, allow as much time as you need or want to experience and investigate each area of the body.

3. Starting with your head, bring your awareness to your body and notice any tension you're feeling as you practise your body-scan meditation. Do you feel tightness anywhere? Pain? A feeling of concentrated 'energy' around a certain area? Sit with it for a minute and notice what you're feeling.

4. When you're ready (no rush), intentionally breathe in and move your attention to whatever part of the body you want to investigate. You might choose to do a systematic body scan, beginning at the head or feet. Or you might choose to explore areas and sensations randomly.

What did my body communicate during my body scan?

....

....

....

....

....

'An emotion
is your body's
reaction to
your mind.'

– Eckhart Tolle

Enjoy the process of chatting to your body! Try to keep learning as much about health and nutrition as you can but remember to listen to what your own body might be trying to tell you. What is right for you may not be right for someone else, so try not to stress too much about following every single piece of advice you've heard about what's healthy. It is your body and you can create wellness that is tailor-made for you.

MONTHLY REVIEW

JOURNAL WORK

When you do notice your body talking to you, my advice is to follow the process below.

1. **Stop and recognise**: simply stop and become aware of how your body is talking to you.

2. **Experience**: fully feel any emotion associated with this.

3. **Tune in and reflect**: practise curiosity with yourself to determine what your body is telling you.

4. **Ask** what your body **really** needs to be healthy, healed and whole. Acknowledge how you feel now.

5. **Name it**: energetic, sluggish, contented, bloated, headache-free, overwhelmed? Can you see or feel a distinct connection between how you feel and what you did that day?

6. **Journal**: when you identify the feeling or message from your body, take a few minutes to write about it. You can even try writing a letter to your body in acknowledgement for the message received.

Dear Body,

Thank you for all the work you do daily to help me live a vibrant life. I realise I need to listen to what you need so we can continue to thrive.

What do you need from me now?

....

....

....

....

....

....

....

....

MEDITATION

This month's meditation is all about tuning into what your body is trying to communicate to you. You can listen and then record your findings in your journal. You will also find a guided body-scan meditation on the website, so make time on your own to try the body-scan exercise. You can find it at Month 10 at www.andreahayes.ie.

My Journal Extract

For a long time I didn't recognise my own alarm signals, especially where work and over-commitment were concerned. I would often get a frog in my throat when I knew I was saying yes to something I should be saying no to. Now that I can decipher my body's signals, my throat constriction acts as a friendly reminder not to over-commit.

However, there has been a switch up recently and I feel I need to reconnect with myself and my body. I am experiencing a whole plethora of new feelings and I need to tune in to what is going on inside for remainder of my pregnancy.

I am so aware of my pain 'sensations' that I have become my best doctor. And becoming pregnant again has really highlighted how effective I have become at managing and communicating with my body, which is all really positive, but the recent flare-up of pain was a sharp reminder to me that I am only human and, despite my best efforts, things can go out of sync.

It is a classic example of a new dimension – the pregnancy is adding more stress to my body so I need to factor that in to how I pace myself and increase self-care. Whenever I get a new pain or a new medical challenge, my current routine needs to be tweaked and I am in that space now. For the next week I am going to try some new routines and monitor and journal about how my body is.

In one way I am kind of in awe of my body – we have achieved the impossible: a viable pregnancy. Please God, may this last, and I know I need to work with my body and help it in every way possible. Feeling blessed.

A x

My Journal

'Put your heart, mind and soul into
even your smallest acts. This is the
secret of success.'
— Swami Sivananda

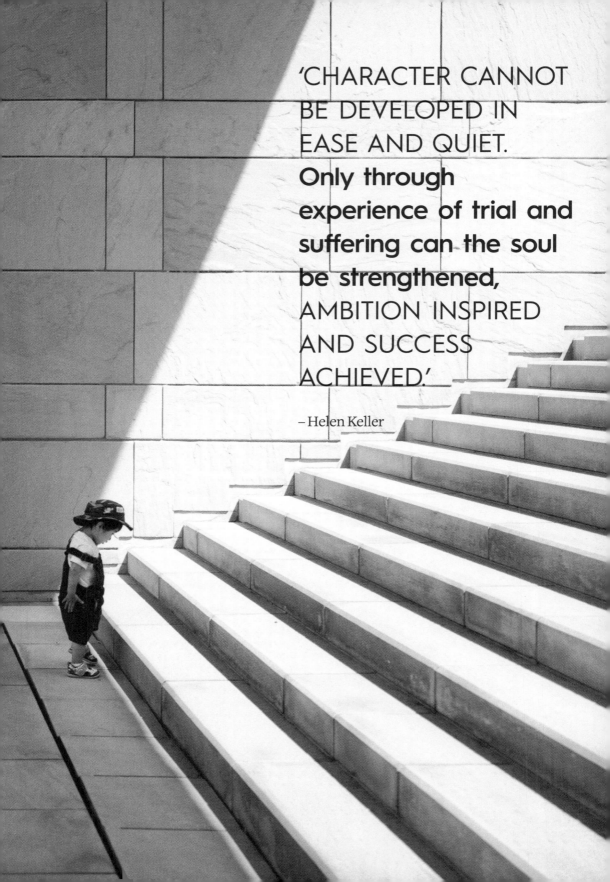

'CHARACTER CANNOT BE DEVELOPED IN EASE AND QUIET. Only through experience of trial and suffering can the soul be strengthened, AMBITION INSPIRED AND SUCCESS ACHIEVED.'

– Helen Keller

MONTH 11

Soul Signature: Mapping Your Desire

'EFFORTS & COURAGE

are not enough without

PURPOSE & DIRECTION.'

– John F. Kennedy

I don't think I am unique in having a burning desire to discover my true calling, my most authentic expression in the world, that unique, distinctive thing I am here to do. It is the 'holy grail' search of humanity – it's like an itch we must scratch, a subtle, abiding awareness that there is something more for us to do on our journey through life. Let's face it, we all want the miraculous power of knowing what it is we are supposed to do that will provide happiness and sustenance to our existence. It is the icing on the complex cake that is life. It is what some people call our **soul signature.**

Have you ever noticed that the people who are living their true expression of themselves seem to have an aura about them, an intriguing quality that draws you in and welcomes you like a moth to a flame? They are irresistibly luminous. You can sense the deep authenticity of their being.

There really isn't a big mystery about what they have. I feel they have simply embraced being exactly who they are – we might say they are comfortable in their own skin. They have balanced mind, body and soul.

DARE OF THE DAY

Take a little time to stop and reflect on who you are and see if you can answer the following question.

How would I describe my soul signature?

....

....

....

....

....

....

Life is a journey with many stops along the way. If we had some idea of what to expect, at least some of the time, it might make things flow more easily. Of course, when we have a map for that journey we can take each day step-by-step towards our destiny.

But sometimes navigating that journey is difficult and often we need to **stop** and accept we have lost our way or are a little off track. This was true for me. You know the feeling: you look around and things are unfamiliar. You are lost, without direction, yet you keep wandering through, hoping to see a signpost to lead you in the right direction.

This is OK, but it can be frustrating, exhausting and time consuming, and often we get further off track, which can sometimes lead us down the path of danger. It might also prove fruitless as, with no direction, you are just meandering through life without focus or purpose.

Maybe you're getting that lost feeling right now in your day-to-day life, in your relationships, your career, your home life, your health, your finances, your spiritual life. Do any of the situations below sound familiar?

✳ You wake up tired, and thinking about the day seems draining, not energising.

✳ You have a feeling that you need something more – things you once enjoyed doing now feel like a burden.

✳ You feel stuck, miserable and uncomfortable; you want change – how you're living doesn't seem to be working anymore.

Soul mapping your heart's desire and creating a new life plan is simple but powerful. You wouldn't think about setting out on a trip without having some idea of where you're going and how to get there. There are specific directions you have to follow. Sometimes we need inspiration and it is OK to look to others for guidance and also to look within for clues to what you truly want.

'I am only but I am **one,** I cannot do everything, but I can do something.'

– Edward Everett Hale

DARE OF THE WEEK

Before you start soul mapping, it's useful to answer the simple questions below. Also, don't be afraid to look to people you know or have read about and consider whether you want to emulate parts of their life's journey for inspiration to put you on the right path.

What qualities would I like to emulate and why?

_____

_____

_____

_____

Look at the different areas in your life: are you off track in any?

_____

_____

_____

_____

What direction is your soul sending you in?

_____

_____

_____

_____

I am asking you to create your own navigation system for your whole life. When you are on the right path, your life flows and seeds are sown on the journey to help manifest new opportunities that you might have never imagined. This map will help you find your way to happiness in your job, home, health, finances and relationships and enable you to keep moving forward with confidence, purpose and intention.

Step by step, you will discover inner passion, purpose, peace, prosperity and love, all by learning how to honour the call of your soul. Forget about your past journey – that road map shows only where you've been, where you've come from to arrive at this moment.

You are here. What is the destination you desire?

In this very moment, imagine, without any limits, being your most magnificent expression of yourself. Everything that has happened in your life has served to bring you to this place. Trust that **anything** is possible.

* Don't worry about how you are going to achieve it.

* Visualise your dream; imagine the best possible outcome: it could be a new job or retirement, a new love or a vocation – whatever you desire.

* See it and believe it. Now write what that vision is.

* The road map for the next leg of your journey starts **now**.

Outline the clear plan for the next leg in the journey of your life.

'THE GOOD LIFE IS A
p r o c e s s,
not a state of being.
IT IS A DIRECTION,
not a destination.'

– Carl Rogers

Setting your own course in life is so important. As we grow older, we sometimes see we have been a passenger on someone else's journey, which can be great for the view, but there is nothing like being in the driving seat.

Research suggests that this becomes more important as we age, and that people who have found a purpose 'larger than themselves' do better because they are more connected to community. Victor Frankl came out of the World War II concentration camps believing you have to create your own meaning for your life. Living for what you believe can make a positive change in the world and helps to put your own life in perspective – it keeps you from getting depressed about the state of the world.

DARE OF THE MONTH

Now is the time to awaken your heart's desire and start your soul journey. Sit into the driver's seat and make your deepest wish a reality; illuminate the world with your unique soul signature. This month, take some time to read the steps below and use this navigation system to journal the new, exciting direction of your life.

STEP 1 – GPS

We all have probably used GPS for directions on many journeys, but do we tune into our own innate GPS? This is your journey, and only you have the internal guidance and information about your true destination, so always listen to your inner voice – it will help you find your way back to that centred place from which all our wisdom comes. Imagine you are a satellite: you need to tune in to pick up the signals and allow your receiver to intercept the messages as they arrive. If you feel you need help, journal about the path ahead before you get started on the journey.

STEP 2 – OPEN ROAD

Don't be afraid to take time to explore alone, go off the beaten track and maybe disappear for a day for a little solitude. Think of an open road – no traffic, no distractions, no cares along the way: it's just you on the road trip, so blast your music loud, sing along and enjoy your journey. Sometimes we need to take time out to tap into our soul's innermost desires and allow those lightbulb moments to guide us along our soul search.

STEP 3 – BYPASS

Avoid, avoid, avoid – your GPS will usually alert you to things that will make your journey longer and keep you stuck in traffic. So start now by bypassing things and people in life that no longer serve you. See this as traffic – it's annoying and it's best avoided if possible. Part of your spiritual development will see you naturally outgrow certain relationships and organically meet new people who are making shifts to live in a more holistic style, as you are. When you get a gut feeling or an inexplicable urge to skip an appointment or a meeting with a friend, or to simply not make time for a person anymore, listen to it. This is your GPS and you need to bypass.

STEP 4 – YIELD

On the road, it is important to proceed with caution and to yield and allow others to go first. Equally, this applies to succeeding on your soul journey in a holistic sense. I believe a good mantra is to respect others' journeys. When in doubt, I suggest applying the courtesy give-way rule. In life we can often get ourselves in trouble by approaching too fast, especially at junctions and roundabouts. We think we know the way but we forget others may decide to cut us off, and these unforeseen actions of others can cause us to crash. So if conditions seem uncertain in life or on your journey, don't be afraid to slow down, let others pass – it is not a race to the finish line. And when your soul craves clarity, proceed with caution – think: is it right? Is it good for me? Is it good for others? Is it good for my journey to react to others' bad behaviour or should I just yield and let them pass?

STEP 5 – SCENIC ROUTE AND DETOURS

You can always take the scenic route and enjoy the sights. Even when we are driving to relocate to a new destination, it doesn't mean it can't be fun and inspiring along the way.

Ask yourself: how are you going to make this journey fun? I am a firm believer in having fun. I think you will do whatever you are doing better if you are enjoying yourself. So don't be afraid to stop on the road to remember the journey so far and enjoy the view. Fun is all about exploration and even experiments – you might fail or lose your way, but if it lights you up then don't be afraid to pursue it. Fun can also be about handling difficult situations or people with levity and laughter.

STEP 6 – ROADBLOCKS

Often in life we encounter things that seem to stop our way forward – at the time we can only see the route from A to B and this jam is stopping us in our tracks. But often there is another road to the same destination and one that is best for us. I had this experience with a pain documentary that I really wanted to pursue. Everything in my being said this was the right path for me, but I kept receiving rejections. My goal was to bring awareness about chronic pain and I couldn't see an alternative until I took the opportunity to stop and take another look at the block ahead. I changed direction and wrote my first book, *Pain-Free Life*. I learned to use these moments as opportunities to tune into my own GPS and navigate another way that speaks to my soul. Your goals may change or a path may branch off into another one you never before considered. Your intuition is like a roadworks sign, flashing at you, alerting you to roadblocks ahead, so pay attention to it and, most importantly, stay alert and journal along your journey. The pages are your mental signposts, bodily vital signs and spiritual breadcrumbs along the way to guide you.

STEP 7 – U-TURNS

You need to master being in the driving seat of your life by taking control and responsibility for your choices. We often ignore the GPS because we think we know a shortcut or the best way forward and sometimes we find ourselves heading in the wrong direction. When that happens there is a simple way solution: make a U-turn.

This ability to admit that you need to rethink your direction will help you to be OK with changing from what you once said, thought or did. It can take courage to say I tried that road and it is no longer right or safe for me now.

I experienced this when I had to reassess my goals and dreams. Sometimes we think we want money, prestige or power and we are driven on a trajectory to attain those, but that path might not be a pleasant one. It takes some soul searching and map adjusting to admit that, although we are on the journey and have committed time and dedication to succeed, it isn't what we truly want. Don't be in the fast lane of future failure: make a change, turn around and start again. Being able to admit you need a U-turn in your life is a sign of the brave, awakened and wise.

STEP 8 – BE CAREFUL WHO YOU PICK UP AND DON'T FORGET TO STOP FOR PEDESTRIANS

As I became more grounded in my true, authentic self and aware of my daily life, I began to become both more grateful and more conscious of the people in my life and crossing paths with me on my journey.

Jim Rohn said, 'You are the average of the five people you spend the most time with.' So pay attention to those close. If your closest relationships are with people who have negative, complaining, begrudging attitudes, then it might be time to offload them on your journey.

Look around and see who the people around you are. Make time to stop and chat to those who seem to love life and want to make a difference – people who are optimistic, who strive for excellence, kindness, fairness. These people don't judge or make excuses – they are the radiators.

Make an effort to think about the greater purpose of people crossing your path in life. Instead of speeding by, slow down, stop and give them your time and attention. Ask yourself, what can I learn from them? What can I teach them?

In order to travel the road to success, you have to find road-trip companions who are going in the same extraordinary direction in which you want to travel.

STEP 9 – OFF-RAMPS AND TIME OUT

There will be crossroads, potholes, flat tyres and dark roads ahead along the way. An exit sign will often appear when something becomes too challenging. It can feel like everything is working against you, but see this as an opportunity to take some time out to refuel, not an opportunity to give up on the journey because you are disheartened or tired.

Don't mistake exiting to refuel for the path ahead as an excuse to give up. A timeout is needed to service your car, so allow yourself time to relax, chill, maybe take a short holiday or just some time to look over your map. Be it an off-ramp in a relationship, business partnership, your health or planning your life ahead, see it as an opportunity to re-examine your direction and approach to your current situation. When you feel like you are driving on empty, don't allow your engine to break down – exit and look for the timeout sign. It's time to take a break from life and allow yourself to rethink the way forward.

STEP 10 - GREEN LIGHT

I'll assume that many of you have done a fair amount of reading in order to understand yourselves better. Or maybe you have spent some time writing or journaling to express your feelings and make sense of what has happened to you. Now I want you to see this moment as your green light to drive forward in the direction of your dreams.

If you want make an actual map in your journal of your journey ahead, you might choose to draw your life complete with physical landmarks, people and places you've been to get you to the point you are at now.

Imagine that this book has been a traffic stop and your light has just turned green. Now is the time: seize the moment, stop waiting for the lights to turn amber and then red! It will be too late then and you will lose your momentum. Drive forward, chase your dreams – put the pedal to the metal and follow your soul map!

If you feel you need an accountability buddy, tell someone you trust about your plans ahead (even writing it in your journal might be enough to keep you on the path ahead). This person will keep you moving forward – they'll sound the horn with a loud *beep beep* when you stop.

Begin today and use the soul map provided or make up your own map to your souls journey in your private journal or writing space. The important thing is to dream big and have fun imagining a wonderful end destination.

SOUL MAP

1. GPS – where is my desired destination?

_____

2. Open Road – what path will I take to get there?

_____

3. Bypass – are there situations or people in my life I need to avoid?

_____

4. Yield – what would I do if I had more time?

_____

5. Scenic Route and Detours – where does my life lack passion?

_____

6. Roadblocks – who is stopping me living on purpose? Maybe that person is me!

7. U-Turns – how can I change direction and go on a new path?

8. Be Careful Who You Pick Up and Don't Forget to Stop for Pedestrians – who are my drains and radiators?

9. Off-Ramps and Time out – retreat and rethink my next move.

10. Green Light – where do I need to GO next?

'Faith is taking the first step, even when you don't see the whole staircase.'

–Martin Luther King, Jr.

MONTHLY REVIEW

JOURNAL WORK

Ask yourself the following **soul questions**.

What is your unique soul signature?

....

....

Look at all the different areas in your life. Are you off track or have you lost direction?

I am on track in:

....

....

I have lost direction in:

....

....

What direction is your soul sending you in?

....

....

MEDITATION

This month's meditation is all about connecting with your true life's purpose and soul signature and mapping your journey ahead.

This meditation will help to anchor you deeply in your true, authentic self and strengthen your soul connection. You can find it at Month 11 at www.andreahayes.ie.

My Journal Extract

I know I write about journeys a lot, and I keep thinking lately about the different paths we can take, but I feel eventually they will bring you to the same place: it just depends on how quickly you reach that point in your 'journey'.

As I walked on my usual path with Dash, I remembered a few months ago a conversation I had with God. I was looking for direction and asking him to show me the way. After the walk I came home to journal in the office and got distracted and started cleaning my library. I picked out a few books – I didn't do anything with them but decided to leave them beside the computer. This morning I found them and one was a book I must have bought years ago on Ignatius and the Daily Examine. I can't remember reading it but I was drawn to it, then a few months ago, again, I pulled it out but still didn't read it. When I saw it today and picked it up, suddenly it made sense.

I am now studying this work through my course but it has been presented to me many times before. I always say, when the student is ready, the teacher will appear, and luckily Fr Myles has been a gift to me in recent years, as he has gently guided me towards this spiritual path – I already had all the material at my fingertips but I just wasn't open to seeing it. So maybe I could have studied this work a few years ago or even a few months ago, but it's all about timing and now feels right. So, too, does the notion that what is meant for you won't pass you.

A x

'There is a Divine Design for each man!
Just as the perfect picture of the oak is in the
acorn, the Divine pattern of his life is in the
superconscious mind of man.'

– Florence Scovel Shinn

My Journal

'The soul which has no fixed purpose
in life is lost; to be everywhere, is to be
nowhere.'
– Michel de Montaigne

'Divine is all
LOVE
in its essential nature,
and love is all Divine in its
truthful expression.'

– Maharishi Mahesh Yogi

MONTH 12

Divine Mind

Philosophers, psychologists, anthropologists, clergy, the best minds from east and west and even ordinary people like you and me have failed to reach the same answer to this age-old question.

What is the self?

Think about the nature of self – what does it mean to you?

* Is it real?
* Is it an illusion?
* Where is it?
* Can you find it?
* Do you always have it?
* Is it just a feeling?
* Is it your personal identity?
* Were you born with it?
* Did it exist before you were born into this world?
* Will your self exist beyond this worldly life?

We frequently throw around terms like self-discovery, self-identity, self-esteem, self-belief, self-control, self-enhancement, self-concept, self-improvement! But when we discuss at length these important phenomena, do we know exactly what **self** in each of those terms really means?

The traditional answer, found in many sources, is that the self is an immortal soul that transcends the physical. However there are many other theories. I think most agree the self does exist but as a highly complex, multi-level system of interacting mechanisms.

Your self-concepts and behaviours all depend in part on the interactions you have with other people, including ones who influence you and also ones from whom you want to differentiate yourself.

'Know thyself,' advised the Delphic oracle,
Greece's version of self-help.

For me, my self is anchored in the body, mind and soul – it's all of these tied into a coherent unit that gives me my sense of wholeness and self.

One of the people and teachers who has greatly influenced my journey to my true self is the late artist, metaphysical writer and spiritual teacher, Florence Scovel Shinn (1871–1940). She was also acknowledged by Louise L. Hay as an early influence, and in my opinion she was far ahead of her time in understanding how to connect the mind, body and spirit to the Divine within.

The recent popularity of the book *The Secret* brought the theme of manifestation to the mainstream, but Florence Scovel Shinn had a profound understanding of how this method works. She writes about it in *Your Word Is Your Wand* (published in 1928). Her understanding of the self and our connection to the Higher Power go hand in hand with her powerful affirmations. For example, when we speak about using visualisation to manifest our dreams, she would affirm:

'Never force a picture by visualising; let the Divine
Idea flash into your conscious mind; then the student is
working according to the Divine Design.'

When we talk about problems, there is nothing that can't be overcome, affirming:

'Divine Love, through me, now dissolves all seeming
obstacles and makes clear, easy and successful my way.'

She denied loss, using this affirmation:

'I deny loss, there is no loss in Divine Mind therefore I
cannot lose that pencil. I will receive it or its equivalent.'

She articulates how we all have a Divine Design and that to know the self is the way to attain the wisdom we need to follow our path in this life. One of her affirmations says:

'In the Divine Design there is no limitation, only health, wealth, love and perfect self-expression.'

DARE OF THE DAY

Write your own affirmations to say daily to invigorate your mind, body and soul. Write until you find something that resonates with you on a deep level. The words will have an energy that is unique to you and this energy will grow when you read them.

Mind:

....

....

....

Body:

....

....

....

Soul:

....

....

....

The Divine self is in relationship with the ever-evolving **I am** awareness within. It is a higher self that transcends the mind, body and soul; it is in every person ever born. It is the essence of the Universe that dwells in your being. By connecting to the source of this light and life within you, you will reveal and embrace your motivation for living an authentic life. It illustrates so many of the cosmic truths that have been discovered by the great mystics of east and west. It is the self that you are in a state of becoming through your evolution, through all of your experiences in time and space. I have been on this journey with you and I believe that to find your true calling is to live in the light of the Divine.

The Divine self is what powers your mind, body and soul and makes you feel awe and wonder. When we are truly in balance these three parts, in a sense, could be called the trinity of your self-identity.

* **Mind:** your mind is ever-aware and has been thinking since you began existing in this lifetime, and since your birth in other lifetimes.

* **Body:** the body and the physical realm, in which we dwell, are thought to be a vehicle for the higher self.

* **Soul:** your soul is the spirit light at your core that chose to be incarnate at this point in time.

> To know oneself (or one's self)
> is in fact a life-long project.

Humanity is awakening and evolving beyond its narrow level of consciousness. Peter N. Borys Jr., author, multidimensional metaphysical teacher, consciousness and energy researcher, dimensional evolutionist and visionary writes:

> 'In our journey to become a higher expression of our
> true consciousness in Divine Being,
> we often use language that includes words such as
> "healing", "transformation", and "evolution"
> to describe a process of change.

We see the journey to a higher consciousness this way because a false awareness of limitation, separation, conflict and external control has been conditioned into our consciousness. We are awakening to the reality that we emanate from Divine Being, and are one with the Divine as love, peace, harmony and creative intelligence. We are Divine Light.'

I believe the purpose of our evolution on earth is to live with unconditional love for the self, grow in self-mastery and balance and fulfil our mission by living in our Divine Light. In this process of awakening, we are elevating our consciousness to the highest and purest frequency of love, wisdom, knowledge and understanding as Divine unique beings.

Maybe it is our human destiny to awaken and experience infinite love in our multidimensional mind, body and soul.

I have grown so deeply while on this journey and I hope that by following the guidance in the pages of this journal you will grow, develop and awaken. It is a healing and transforming process. As we work through our layers to self, all traumas and conditioning in the mind, body and soul from a lifetime of rejection, loss, fear, conflict, control and separation will be transcended. We are clearing any historical conditioned patterns in the subconscious and beginning to open up fully and lovingly to the full capacities of the true self.

When we find this balance, the wholeness of our self radiates powerful frequencies of the infinite higher Divine – this is our true nature and in this sweet spot all things are possible, but you have to do the work.

We need to clearly set our intention to make contact with our Divine self, to open to it and receive the unlimited energy, love, inspiration and all the transformation, awareness and gifts of consciousness it is always offering the self. The fact that you are here now reading these words means you are receptively on the journey to making this connection and to receive guidance, energy and inspiration.

'The DIVINE
is not something high above us.
It is in heaven, it is in earth,
it is inside us.'

– Morihei Ueshiba

DARE OF THE WEEK

How can you bring your whole self (mind, body and soul) forward to live each day with **passion and purpose**?

* ✳ Clear your energy and set your self-inquiry intention.
* ✳ Silence is a vital factor in this process.
* ✳ Let go of thoughts and connect with your **I am**.
* ✳ Calling upon your Divine self, ask the **soul questions** below.
* ✳ Listen and be receptive to the insights and messages.
* ✳ Journal afterwards and this will provide guidance.
* ✳ Trust.

What is your passion?

....

....

....

....

What is your purpose?

....

....

....

....

What pursuits ignite your passion and purpose?

....

....

....

....

....

What steps can you take today to bring you closer to your passion and purpose?

....

....

....

....

....

The answers may come as an instinct, insight, a vision or a knowingness, or a new path may open up, a new opportunity may come to you, a teacher may show up, a new person may enter your life or something or someone is withdrawn from your path; you may receive a new understanding, a feeling of peace and harmony. There are multiple ways your Divine self connects with you and only you will be able to understand what this means for you. Remain open for the response in whatever way it may come to you.

I promise that doing this brings more power, love, wisdom, guidance, abundance and spiritual vision, insight, extra energy and inspiration – everything you need will be imparted to you and will unfold at the perfect time to show you the light.

When I reflected on my journey, I could see how I had turned many past hurts into healing lessons, and I could see how my reactions to people and situations had changed. This new way of being might take a little adjusting to, but when we reflect on our lessons we will see which chapters have been our biggest teachers.

For me, I need to remember to cultivate my passion for altruism – this is something I try to work on daily. My own personal journey of study to become a spiritual companion really fills me with a great sense of purpose.

The act of holding a space for another person and truly listening to them is very special. When you send loving kindness, empathy, compassion, peace, generosity, grace and pure love to another, you are not only giving that energy out, you are also integrating those same qualities into your own life, and I have found I am cultivating more benevolence, unconditional love and divinity in my own world.

So whatever it is you want to become your purpose, enhance the feelings that stimulate your passion, nurture that energy, repeat those feelings, preserve the image of your passion in your heart and allow your mind to enhance them so the feelings will gradually fill your world and your mental landscape in a more meaningful way.

'Divine **LOVE** always has been, and always will be, the answer that you seek.'

– Doreen Virtue

DARE OF THE MONTH

If you still don't know what your true calling is then simply start by doing these three things for this next month.

1. COUNT YOUR BLESSINGS

It seems simplistic, but the more you focus on all that is good in your life, the more that good energy expands. Stop wishing your time away with 'when I have ... I will be happy': be happy now and enjoy the simple pleasures in the everyday. We have so many gifts to be thankful for, so start listing everything you are grateful for every day and see how this easy daily habit will start to reveal all the positives in your life.

2. WATCH THE COMPANY YOU KEEP

Sometimes our own sense of purpose can stem from the people we surround ourselves with. Have a look around and see if you are with drains or radiators. Do the people in your life inspire you or could you change the company you keep and meet more interesting likeminded people? Remember, your vibe attracts your tribe.

3. WRITE

Meditating and writing can help you find your purpose. Keep journaling and asking your soul those meaningful questions. Get into the daily habit of sitting in silence and checking in with yourself. When you couple this with a little journaling, your life, I believe, can truly change and things become so much clearer.

See yourself through a lens of unconditional love and perfection. When we return to our mind, body and soul oneness with the Divine self within, we have truly found our sacred magical place in this Universe and our world is full of endless possibilities. When you connect with the Divine life force within, you will sense a connection to the universal life force of all living things – there is no separation.

For me, it was the realisation that everything I needed was within me.

'The kingdom of heaven is "WITHIN" or "AMONG" us'

– Luke 17:21

MONTHLY REVIEW

JOURNAL WORK

Soul questions to ask your Divine self:

How can I open my heart and release any thoughts or feelings that are less than loving to myself and others?

_____

_____

What do I need to release that is keeping me stuck or unable to move forward on my higher path in life?

_____

_____

What doubts or distractions or people are keeping me from my higher path?

_____

_____

What is holding me back and keeping me from seeing my next steps on this journey to embrace being my Divine self?

_____

_____

Think of anything else and ask – there is nothing your Divine self cannot answer.

_____

_____

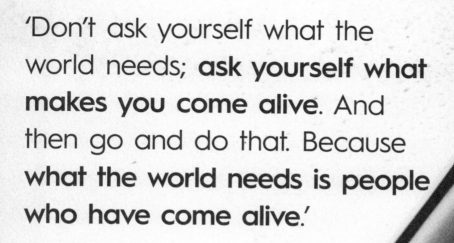

'Don't ask yourself what the world needs; **ask yourself what makes you come alive**. And then go and do that. Because **what the world needs is people who have come alive**.'

– Harold Whitman

TIPS TO REMEMBER

    ✻ Love yourself unconditionally.

    ✻ Let go of expectations.

    ✻ Surrender and release attachment to the way you think things should be.

    ✻ Quiet the voice of your ego so you can hear the voice of inner wisdom
       of **I am**.

    ✻ Forgive yourself and others.

    ✻ Understand the shadow – it might be scary but face uncertainty
       with faith.

    ✻ Embrace your emotions and lovingly acknowledge them.

    ✻ Ignite your light through awareness and creativity.

    ✻ Centre yourself in your vibration and energy.

    ✻ Listen to your body and look to nature as a teacher.

    ✻ Decide on a new direction and begin the journey.

    ✻ Open up to your true nature – remember being of service reveals the
       Divine plan in our lives in often-unexpected ways.

MEDITATION

This month's meditation is about expanding your higher consciousness and sense of self. You will be guided on a journey that reveals your evolution. During the meditation, there will be silent spaces for you to reflect and connect with the very core of your being. You can find it at Month 12 at www.andreahayes.ie.

'Go
CONFIDENTLY
in the direction of your
DREAMS.
Live the life you have
IMAGINED.'

– Henry David Thoreau

My Journal Extract

Nature is such a tonic. As I took my daily walk today, I realised I felt so blissful – for no particular reason, I was feeling grounded, serene, peaceful, balanced, happy, blessed and just wonderfully aligned to myself.

I began to think about this energy and how I could almost bottle it and feel this way all the time. Nothing was different – obviously I am pregnant and I feel so blessed about that miracle, but other than that it is a normal Tuesday and I feel so happy.

I think I have woken up to my own awareness. In my own journey of growth and development, I've learned that I experience this amazing feeling of connection and balance in my mind, body and soul and to the Universe itself and to the source of all things Divine when I am willing to set aside time to tune in to myself in meditation and, lately, the practice of the Ignatius daily examine prayer. I have expanded spiritually and consciously when I have taken action on the guidance I receive during these moment of prayer and reflection. The habit of asking for light, looking for that guidance, being grateful, reviewing my day with grace, looking ahead to tomorrow, trying to do a little better than today and just living in the moment is keeping me in this bubble of bliss and I love it. I watch my moods and emotions become charged and I choose to engage or just watch them dissipate with loving energy.

I know how easy it is to become ungrounded and stressed so I want to remember today – the simple walk, but most of all the feeling of serenity, and I need to lock the feeling into my cells so I can recall it in meditation and return to it when I needed. I feel at one, whole, ignited, switched on, blessed, loved and in love.

A x

My Journal

'There is no greater gift you can give
or receive than to honor your calling.
It's why you were born. And how you
become most truly alive.'
— Oprah Winfrey

'IF YOU CAN'T FIGURE OUT YOUR PURPOSE, FIGURE OUT YOUR *passion.* FOR YOUR PASSION WILL LEAD YOU RIGHT INTO YOUR *purpose.*'

– Bishop T. D. Jakes

Final Thoughts – Review, Reflect, Revise

MIND

Accept and appreciate your amazing mind: it is your most powerful tool and has the capability to transform your life. I know from my personal healing journey that the mind can heal – and thanks to modern neuroscience there is no more hiding from this fact.

It can be called spontaneous remission, the placebo effect or miracle healing, but we know that the persistent and consistent practice of feeding the mind, body and soul with positive thoughts and unconditional love can have a healing effect, and it has been proven that with total belief and trust in the process, you can achieve great results.

Researchers like Bruce Lipton, Ph.D. have shown that our thoughts, whether conscious or not, have a profound impact on our bodies – right down to the cellular level and our DNA. It has been proven that when we harbour negative energy towards ourselves with self-limiting beliefs and self-talk, our sense of self and our overall wellness and health will suffer. Fortunately, the reverse is also true.

Remember: every thought counts – choose them wisely, and don't allow your brain to be a hoarder of negative energy.

BODY

We have one beautiful body, one vessel to carry us through life: make sure you are the pilot navigating its path ahead. This body cannot be divided or separated from you.

I believe that within our own bodies, we have an omnipresent all-wise, all-knowing, all-powerful DNA code unlimited in its ability to heal and restore if we listen to it and stay in conversation with it at all times.

It is time to start a loving relationship with your body today. Begin the love affair by honouring it with nourishing foods and living a healthy lifestyle of balance and harmony. We are intuitive and know instinctively what we truly need. This is your Divine body, praise it and love it exactly as it is in this moment – it has carried you every step of this journey.

My relationship with my body changed when I stopped seeing and focusing on my pain and limitations and started to see how strong it actually was: despite all the pain, it kept going, never giving up. This incredible body blessed me with two beautiful children, despite all my challenges, and once I began to hold an inner image of how perfectly brilliant my body was, it became even more invincible.

Start today by holding firm to an inner picture of your perfect body, perfectly healthy and perfectly sized. If you have health goals, be gentle with yourself as you set about achieving them. Align your intentions with those health goals. Pay closer attention to the magical way your body is speaking to you and I promise you will manifest better health.

SOUL

In my own spiritual journey, I've learned that I experience my connection to the source when I am willing to set aside time to tune in through meditation and prayer. I have grown the most spiritually when I have taken action on the guidance I receive – even when it does not always make sense, and even when others may not understand.

Talk with the soul. Throughout the day, ask your questions either in your head or aloud. Build a relationship with the Divine source within your soul where we are all connected to the Higher Power – understand there is no separation between the Divine and you: everything you need is within you. This journey for me was an inside-out one. Instead of looking to the outside world for guidance or wisdom, tap into the eternal source of knowingness that is inside the unique sacred place that only you can journey to – your soul.

Only you know the true essence of you, and when you are aligned to that energy you are in a state of pure bliss – I call it my little bubble. Go there, bask in the energy of wholeness and oneness and don't allow anyone to burst your bubble.

Remember to transcend the ego and other people's expectations of who you should be or how you should be living your life. When you are living your truth, you are awake to all of life's blessings; you enrol and sign up for every experience, stamping your authentic soul signature on everything you do.

Love,

Andrea x

'IN THE END THESE THINGS
MATTER MOST:
HOW WELL DID YOU
LOVE?
HOW FULLY DID YOU
LIVE?
HOW DEEPLY DID YOU
LET GO?'

– Siddhãrtha Gautama

Mindfulness BREAKTHROUGH

Hypnosis **EMOTIONS** CREATIVITY

INTROSPECTION Reframing

MIND**ATTITUDE**

Autosuggestions

VISUALISATION *POSITIVE SELF-TALK*

Meditation AWARENESS

Tuning in to signals Rituals

Balance TRANSFORMATION

SENSES BODY Exercise

SLEEP DIET

INTUITIVE EATING Lifestyle SENSATIONS

CONNECTION Vibes HABIT

Body talk Training Walking